25 need-to-know management ratios

Ciaran Walsh and Stuart Warner

PEARSON

Harlow, England • London • New York • Boston • San Francisco • Toronto • Sydney
Auckland • Singapore • Hong Kong • Tokyo • Seoul • Taipei • New Delhi
Cape Town • São Paulo • Mexico City • Madrid • Amsterdam • Munich • Paris • Milan

Pearson Education Limited
Edinburgh Gate
Harlow CM20 2JE
United Kingdom
Tel: +44 (0)1279 623623
Web: www.pearson.com/uk

First edition published 2015 (print and electronic)

© Pearson Education Limited 2015 (print and electronic)

ISBN: 978–1–292–01639–9 (print)
      978–1–292–01641–2 (PDF)
      978–1–292–01640–5 (eText)
      978–1–292–01642–9 (ePub)

British Library Cataloguing-in-Publication Data
A catalogue record for the print edition is available from the British Library

Library of Congress Cataloging-in-Publication Data
Walsh, Ciaran.
   25 need-to-know manage[ment ratios / Ciaran Walsh and Stuart Warner.]
     pages cm
   Includes index.
   ISBN 978-1-292-01639-9 [(print)—ISBN 978-1-292-01641-2 (PDF)—ISBN 978-1-292-01642-9 (ePub)]
01640-5 (eText)—ISBN 978- [292-01642-9 (ePub)]
   1. Ratio analysis.   2. Mar[...] methods.[...] Warner, Stuart.
II. Title. III. Title: Twenty-fi[ve ...]
   HF5681.R25W14 2015
   658.001'512924--dc23

10 9 8 7 6 5 4 3 2 1
19 18 17 16 15

Cover design by Two Associ[ates]

Print edition typeset in 9pt [StoneSerif by ...]
Print in Great Britain by Ashford Colour Press Ltd, Gosport, Hants

NOTE THAT ANY PAGE CROSS REFERENCES REFER TO THE PRINT EDITION

Contents

About the authors

Ciaran Walsh was formerly Senior Finance Specialist at the Irish Management Institute, Dublin.

Ciaran trained both as an economist and an accountant (BSc (Econ) London, CIMA) and had 15 years' industrial experience before joining the academic world.

His work with senior managers over many years has enabled him to develop his own unique approach to training in corporate finance. As a consequence, he has lectured in most European countries, the Middle East and Eastern Europe.

His main research interest is to identify and computerise the links that tie corporate growth and capital structure into stockmarket valuation.

Ciaran lives in Dublin and is married with six children.

You can contact Ciaran via email at ciaranwalsh@eircom.net

Stuart Warner is a chartered accountant, author, non-executive adviser and trainer.

Stuart delivers finance-based training programmes around the world to both finance and non-finance professionals. Over his career, Stuart has taught thousands of trainee accountants to pass their professional exams for six different accounting qualifications. He has helped thousands of qualified accountants keep up to date and meet their CPD qualifications as well as training many people from non-finance backgrounds to understand financial matters.

Stuart's goal is to help businesses increase productivity and profits through innovative and engaging finance training.

He is a keen advocate of experiential-based learning using business simulations.

He is the author of *Finance Basics* (Collins 'Business Secrets' series); *Making Budgeting Work in the Real World* (NelsonCroom); and co-author of *Dragons' Den: Grow Your Business,* which supports the BBC's *Dragons' Den* programme.

Stuart is a graduate of management sciences from UMIST and became a chartered accountant whilst working at PriceWaterhouseCoopers.

You can find Stuart on LinkedIn or at:
www.financial-fluency.co.uk
or via email at:
kmr@financial-fluency.co.uk

Introduction

The sum and substance of business finance consists of a relatively small number of essential financial measures by means of which we can appraise the success of any commercial enterprise.

These measures are derived from relationships that exist between various financial parameters in the business. While each measure in itself is simple to calculate, comprehension lies not in how to do the calculations but in understanding what these results mean and how the results of different measures mesh together to give a picture of the health of a company.

Why do you need this book?

Business ratios are the guiding stars for the management of enterprises; they provide their targets and standards. They are helpful to managers in directing them towards the most beneficial long-term strategies as well as towards effective short-term decision-making.

Conditions in any business operation change day by day and, in this dynamic situation, the ratios inform management about the most important issues requiring their immediate attention. By definition the ratios show the connections that exist between different parts of the business. They highlight the important interrelationships and the need for a proper balance between departments. A knowledge of the main ratios, therefore, will enable managers of different functions to work more easily together towards overall business objectives.

The common language of business is finance. Therefore, the most important ratios are those that are financially based. The manager will, of course, understand that the financial numbers are only a reflection of what is actually happening and that it is the reality not the ratios that must be managed.

The power of illustrations

This book is different from the majority of business books. You will see where the difference lies if you flip through the pages. It is not so much a text as a series of lectures captured in print – a major advantage of a good lecture being the visual supports.

It is difficult and tedious to try to absorb a complex subject by reading straight text only. Too much concentration is required and too great a load is placed on the memory. Indeed, it takes great perseverance to continue on to the end of a substantial text. It also takes a lot of time, and spare time is the one thing that busy managers do not have in quantity.

Diagrams and illustrations, on the other hand, add great power, enhancing both understanding and retention. They lighten the load and speed up progress. Furthermore, there is an elegance and form to this subject that can only be revealed by using powerful illustrations.

Managers operating in today's ever more complex world have to assimilate more and more of its rules. They must absorb a lot of information quickly. They need effective methods of communication. This is the logic behind the layout of this book.

The approach

There are many, many business ratios and each book on the subject gives a different set – or, at least, they look different.

We see a multitude of names, expressions and definitions, a myriad of financial terms and relationships, and this is bewildering. Many who make an attempt to find their way through the maze give up in despair.

The approach taken in this book is to ignore many ratios initially in order to concentrate on the 25 that are vital. The reason for their importance, their method of calculation, the standards we should expect from them and, finally, their interrelationships will be explored.

The subject is noted for the multitude of qualifications and exceptions to almost every rule. It is these that cause confusion, even though, quite often, they are unimportant to the manager. They are often there because they have an accounting or legal importance. Many statements will be made that are 95% true – the 5% that is left unsaid being of importance only to the specialist.

The philosophy

All commercial enterprises use money as a raw material which they must pay for. Accordingly, they have to earn a return sufficient to meet these payments. Enterprises that continue to earn a return sufficient to pay the market rate for funds usually prosper. Those enterprises that fail over a considerable period to meet this going market rate usually do not survive – at least not in the same form and under the same ownership.

This golden rule cannot be overemphasised, and an understanding of its implications is vital to successful commercial operations. This is true for individual managers as well as for whole communities.

The excitement

Not only is this subject important for the promotion of the economic well-being of individuals and society, it is also exciting – it has almost become the greatest sport. Business provides all the thrills and excitement that competitive humankind craves. The proof of this is that the thrusts and counter-thrusts of entrepreneurs provide regular headlines in our daily press.

This book will link the return on financial resources into day-to-day operating parameters of the business. It will give these skills to managers from all backgrounds. The objective is that all business functions such as production, marketing and distribution can exercise their specialist skills towards the common goal of financial excellence in their organisations.

Data that make sense

Managers, indeed, all of us, are deluged with business data. We see data in internal operating reports, the daily press, business magazines and many other sources. Much of this data is incomprehensible. We know the meaning of the words used separately, but, used collectively, they can be mystifying. Figure I.1 illustrates the problem. The individual words 'shares', 'profits' and 'cash flow' are familiar to us, but we are not sure how they fit together to determine the viability of the business and articles written about the subject are not much help – they seem to come up with a new concept each month.

Is it possible to make the separate pieces shown in (a) into a coherent, comprehensive picture, as shown in (b)? The answer, for the most part, is 'yes'.

The big issues in business are:

- assets
- profits
- cash flow
- growth.

These four variables have interconnecting links. There is a balance that can be maintained between them and, from this balance, corporate value is created. It is corporate value that is the reason for most business activity and, for this reason, this book focuses on the business ratios that determine corporate value.

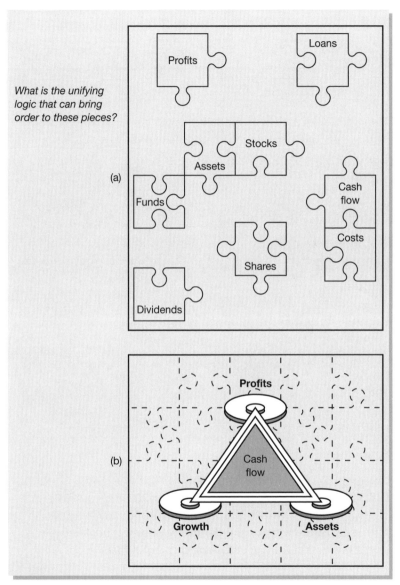

What is the unifying logic that can bring order to these pieces?

Figure I.1   Fitting data together for decision-making

Top 5 do's and don'ts of using financial ratios

Top 5 do's

1. Do: use the right benchmarks

A ratio is meaningless and potentially misleading on its own. To interpret a ratio properly it is essential to use an appropriate benchmark.

Suitable benchmarks can be from internal or external sources. Internally: historic data or another product, service, customer or geographical territory make the best benchmarks. Externally: competitor information (if obtainable), industry data, external analyst reports and government statistics can be useful.

Be careful when comparing to the industry norm. This will be an average and include some extreme top performers and extreme poor performers which may distort the average. It is better to compare against a pre-selection of known good performers which provide the best comparison against your business.

At the same time it is important to remember that no two businesses are the same even if they are direct competitors in the same industry. They could be financed differently and have different tax rates, for example.

2. Do: use an appropriate number of ratios

There is a common desire for businesses to focus on one key ratio. In this book we talk about one of the most popular sole measures, 'return on equity' (Chapters 5 and 12). However, by focusing on one ratio there is a danger of missing out the essential feedback provided by using a variety of ratios.

Whereas it is useful to have a 'primary' ratio, using a portfolio of supporting 'secondary' ratios provides a fuller picture of a business. Additionally, 'secondary' ratios can help to 'read between the lines' and make sure the whole organisation is performing optimally.

A useful analogy is a car dashboard where the speedometer is the primary focus (or key ratio). However, the fuel gauge, tachometer, odometer, oil temperature, oil pressure and engine warning lights provide other essential information which affects the performance of the car.

At the other end of the scale is the symptom of 'analysis paralysis' where businesses monitor so many ratios that it is difficult to 'see the wood for the trees', let alone spot the primary measure.

Returning to the dashboard analogy, many non-pilots would find it challenging to navigate an instrument panel within the cockpit of a modern aircraft.

3. Do: consider timing issues

The financial statements on which many ratios are based are produced at a point in time. The balance sheet (covered in Chapter 2) is a snapshot of the business on a particular day. The position may be different the day before or the day after.

Therefore, it is important to look at trends in ratios versus interpreting ratios at a single point in time.

Seasonality may impact certain businesses. For example a calendar retailer will have high inventory as they build up stocks towards the year-end and hopefully low inventory by the time it gets to February.

Ratios can be influenced by a one-off event. For example, sale of a large asset prior to a company's year-end may boost its bank balance temporarily.

Similarly, there may be a lag in results. A company may have raised debt to fund a sound and profitable investment which will not payback for a number of years.

Additionally, consider the impact of inflation on a company's results. Inflation will impact the analysis of a business's historical results over time. Ratios which indicate improved performance may tell a different story after adjusting for inflation.

Inflation will also impact the analysis of businesses of different ages, who may have purchased similar assets at different times. These assets may be shown at completely different values in each business.

4. Do: check the source of your data

When calculating internal ratios it is important to check the reliability and strength of the business's accounting systems. A small calculation error in one part of the system can be magnified when compounded throughout the whole system. Additionally, when source data are contained in spreadsheets there can be an increased risk of errors.

If calculating ratios on external businesses, check if their accounts have been audited and if they have a clean audit report. Review their accounting policies, such as depreciation which will impact on ratios. Similarly look for changes in accounting policy which will impact the comparison of ratios across years. Be aware that financial statements can include assumptions, judgements and estimations. In addition, changes in accounting standards may impact on comparisons across financial years.

Financial statements are based on book (or historical) values, which may not reflect current reality. This is especially an issue for asset-based ratios. For example, the age of assets, their last revaluation date or if they have been revalued at all, should be considered.

Unethical companies can potentially take advantage of timing issues in what is referred to as 'window dressing', in order to create a desired ratio or even trend. These companies may be tempted to massage figures around their year-end when accounts are produced.

For example, by delaying payments to suppliers at the year-end will increase both year-end cash and accounts payable balances.

5. Do: think twice

It is important to try to 'read between the lines'. Ratios are not definitive measures and need to be interpreted carefully.

Ratios' ability to simplify complex analysis is one of their biggest strengths. However, it can also be their main weakness. As ratios reduce complex data to a single number, they can sometimes miss the bigger picture and potentially give the wrong impression.

If ratios are used in a mechanical, unthinking manner they can lead to incorrect interpretations (or the ones the PR team want you to believe!). However, if ratios are used intelligently they can provide useful insights into a business's performance.

When presented with pre-prepared ratios it is important to check how the ratio has been calculated. Different businesses may calculate the same ratio in different ways. For example, in Chapter 9 we cover three different ways to calculate the popular debt to equity ratio.

Top 5 don'ts

1. Don't: rely on the past to predict the future

It is widely understood that past performance may not be an indicator of future performance.

The financial statements on which ratios are based are a reflection of the past as opposed to the present or even future situation. Therefore, ratios may be based on data which is out of date and not relevant to the future.

2. Don't: rely on a rule of thumb

A good ratio for one business could be a poor ratio for another. A wide diversity of conditions exist in different types of business.

For example (as covered in Chapter 8), some businesses are able to exist comfortably with liquidity ratios that would spell disaster for others. Some businesses have to carry large stocks, have long production cycles and give long credit. Other businesses carry almost no stock and receive more credit than they give.

Strong liquidity in a high growth company could be interpreted as a positive sign. It could also be interpreted as a sign that the company is past the growth phase and this should be reflected in its valuation.

A high asset turnover ratio (covered in Chapter 6) may indicate efficient use of assets or may be indicative of an under-capitalised business which cannot afford to replace its assets.

Financial ratios are useful for analysing a business over time, for example, spotting a fall in profit margin. However, they can be less useful when comparing one business with another, despite their popularity. Differences in accounting policies and practice, for example depreciation rates, or companies that buy versus those that lease equipment, will make it more challenging to compare one business with another.

3. Don't: expect ratios to tell you why something has happened

Ratios are a useful indicator of business performance. However, they indicate *what* has happened but not *why* it has happened. Although ratios can identify changes, there is no indication of the cause of these changes. Correlation does not imply causality.

Further analysis is therefore required in order to determine the cause of a trend. For example, an increase in accounts receivable days (see Chapter 8 on short-term liquidity) could be caused by an increase in sales, a change in credit policy, employee inexperience or potential customer dissatisfaction. It is not possible to reverse a trend until its cause is understood. Only then can the appropriate action be taken.

4. Don't: just use financial ratios

Financial ratios and the financial accounts on which they are based are only part of the story. They cannot give a full picture of a whole business and its performance.

Non-financial ratios, often referred to as 'key performance indicators', are just as if not more important than financial ratios. They help to give a fuller understanding of the whole business. Customer satisfaction, internal processes, product/service quality, employee morale are all important performance measures which should be balanced against financial ratios.

Financial ratios are a great starting point for analysing business performance. However, further, wider and more balanced analysis is required to make informed decisions.

5. Don't: use ratios to replace good management

Ratios should be seen as the starting point for further in-depth analysis. They are a great top-down tool and can be used to facilitate management-by-exception, however, they are just the start of the process.

Ratios are simply a tool and not a substitute for good management. Management is not a numbers game. You cannot run a business using ratios alone. Ratios should not be used mechanically. They cannot replace sound business sense and good judgement.

In turn, when analysing a business, financial ratios cannot measure the quality and experience of managers, although, in the long run, they may reflect management decisions and actions.

part

one

Foundations

Introduction to financial statements

This chapter will introduce you to three key documents:

- The balance sheet
- The profit and loss account
- The cash flow statement

Introduction

To have a coherent view of how a business performs, it is necessary, first, to have an understanding of its component parts. This job is not as formidable as it appears at first sight, because:

- much of the subject is already known to managers, who will have come in contact with many aspects of it in their work;
- while there are, in all, hundreds of components, there are a relatively small number of vital ones;
- even though the subject is complicated, it is based on common sense and can, therefore, be reasoned out once the ground rules have been established.

This last factor is often obscured by the language used. A lot of jargon is spoken and, while jargon has the advantage of providing a useful shorthand way of expressing ideas, it also has the effect of building an almost impenetrable wall around the subject that excludes or puts off the non-specialist. One of the main aims of this book is to show the common sense and logic that underlies all the apparent complexity.

Fundamental to this level of understanding is the recognition that, in finance, there are just three key documents from which we can obtain the vast majority of raw data for our analysis. These are:

- the balance sheet
- the profit and loss account
- the cash flow statement.

A description of each of these, together with their underlying logic, follows.

The balance sheet (B/S)

The balance sheet can be looked on as an engine with a certain mass/weight that generates power output in the form of profit. It is a useful analogy that demonstrates how a balance sheet of a given mass of assets must produce a minimum level of profit to be efficient.

But what is a balance sheet? It is simply an instant 'snapshot' of the assets used by the company and of the funds that are related to those assets. It is a static document relating to one point in time. We therefore take repeated 'snapshots' at fixed intervals – months, quarters, years – to see how the assets and funds change with the passage of time.

The balance sheet is the basic document of account. Traditionally it was always laid out as shown in Figure 1.1, i.e. it consisted of two columns that were headed, respectively, 'Assets' and 'Liabilities'. (Note that the word 'Funds' was often used together with or in place of 'Liabilities'.)

Assets	Liabilities/Funds	
Things owned	**Amounts owed**	Traditional form of balance sheet in two columns.
by the business	by the business	This format will be used in this publication for illustrative
$1,000	$1,000	purposes and to aid understanding.

Figure 1.1   The balance sheet – traditional layout

Assets and liabilities

The 'Assets' column contains, simply, a list of items of value owned by the business.

Assets are mainly shown in the accounts at their cost. Therefore the 'Assets' column is a list of items of value at their present cost to the company. It can be looked on as a list of items of continuing value on which money has been used or spent.

The 'Liabilities' column simply lists the various sources of this same sum of money.

These sources are essentially amounts due to third parties, including the owners.

The company is a legal entity separate from its owners, therefore, the term 'liability' can be used in respect of amounts due from the company to its owners.

The amounts in these columns of course add up to the same total, because the company must identify exactly where funds were obtained from to acquire the assets.

All cash brought into the business is a source of funds, while all cash paid out is a use of funds. A balance sheet can, therefore, be looked on from this angle – as a statement of sources and uses of funds (see Figure 1.2).

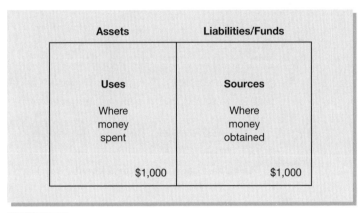

Figure 1.2   The balance sheet – sources and uses of funds approach

The style now used is a single-column layout (see Figure 4.2). This new layout has some advantages, but it does not help the newcomer to understand the logic or structure of the document. For this reason, the two-column layout is mainly used in this publication.

A snapshot

The balance sheet gives a snapshot of the company assets at an instant in time, e.g. 12 o'clock midnight on 31 December 2014.

Further snapshots will be taken at fixed intervals. After each interval the sums recorded against the various components of the balance sheet will have changed.

An analysis of these changes gives crucial information about the company's activities over the period in question.

The profit and loss (P/L) account

The profit and loss account measures the gains or losses from operations over a period of time. It measures total income and deducts total cost.

Both income and cost are calculated according to strict accounting rules. The majority of these rules are obvious and indisputable, but a small number are less so. Even though founded on solid theory, they can sometimes, in practice, produce results that appear nonsensical. These accounting rules are subject to regular review as they attempt to reflect changes in the global economy and business practice.

The profit and loss account quantifies and explains the gains or losses of the company over the period of time bounded by the two balance sheets.

It derives some values from both balance sheets. Therefore it is not independent of them.

It is not possible to alter a value in the profit and loss account without some corresponding adjustment to the balance sheet. In this way the profit and loss account and balance sheet support one another.

The cash flow (C/F) statement

The statement of cash flow is a very powerful document. Cash flows into the company from actual receipts and it flows out when actual payments are made. An understanding of the factors that cause these flows is fundamental.

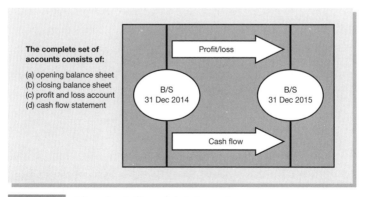

Figure 1.3   Three basic financial statements

The cash flow statement depends on the two balance sheets and the profit and loss account.

It links together the significant elements of all three, so that even though its inclusion in the set of accounts is the most recent in time, it is now regarded in some quarters as the most important.

Summary

These three statements are not independent of each other, but are linked in the system, as shown in Figure 1.3. Together they give a full picture of the financial affairs of a business. We will look at each of these in greater detail.

2

The balance sheet

This chapter will divide the balance sheet into five major blocks:

- Fixed assets
- Current assets
- Owners' funds
- Long-term loans
- Current liabilities

Balance sheet structure

Figure 2.1 shows the balance sheet divided into five major blocks or boxes. These five subsections can accommodate practically all the items that make up the total document. Two of these blocks are on the assets side and three go to make up the liabilities side.

Almost every item that can appear on a balance sheet will fit into one of these boxes. Each box can then be totalled and we now have a balance sheet that consists of five numbers only. These five numbers will tell us much about the company's structure.

We will continually come back to this five-box structure, so it is worthwhile becoming comfortable with it, as we go through each box in turn.

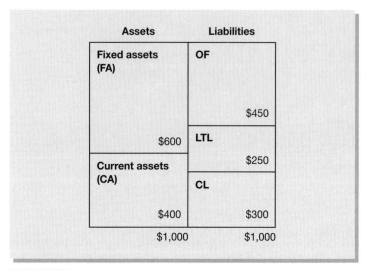

Figure 2.1   The balance sheet – basic five-box layout

We use this five-box balance sheet for its clarity and simplicity. It will be seen later how powerful a tool it is for cutting through the complexities of corporate finance and explaining what business ratios really mean.

Let us look first at the two asset blocks. These are respectively called:

- fixed assets (FA)
- current assets (CA).

These can also be considered as 'long-term' and 'short-term' types of assets. We will see that while this distinction is important in the case of assets, it is even more significant in the case of funds.

Current assets (CA)

This box in the bottom left corner contains all the short-term assets in the company. By short-term we mean that they will normally convert back into cash quickly, i.e. in a period of less than 12 months.

The various items that find their home in this box can be gathered together under four headings:

▪ inventories (stocks)
▪ accounts receivable (trade debtors)
▪ cash
▪ miscellaneous current assets.

These items (see Figure 2.2) are in constant movement. Inventories of raw materials are converted into finished goods. These when sold are transformed into accounts receivable which in due course are paid in cash to the company.

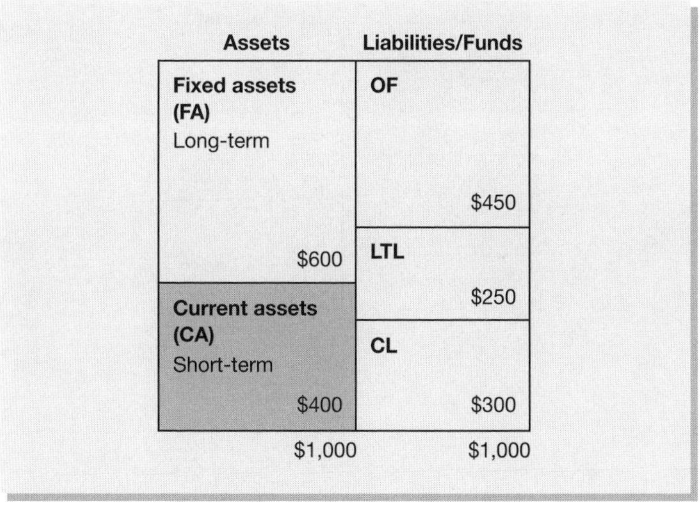

Assets	Liabilities/Funds
Fixed assets (FA) Long-term	**OF**
	$450
$600	**LTL**
	$250
Current assets (CA) Short-term	**CL**
$400	$300
$1,000	$1,000

Figure 2.2 The balance sheet – current assets box

The 'miscellaneous' heading covers any short-term assets not included elsewhere and is usually not significant. The amount of cash held is often small also, because it is not the function of a company to hold cash. Indeed, where there are large cash balances, there is usually a very specific reason for this, such as a planned acquisition.

The two significant items in current assets therefore are the inventories and accounts receivable. They are very important assets that often amount to 50% of the total balance sheet of the company.

Fixed assets (FA)

Fixed assets comprise the second major block of assets. They occupy the top left corner of the balance sheet (see Figure 2.3).

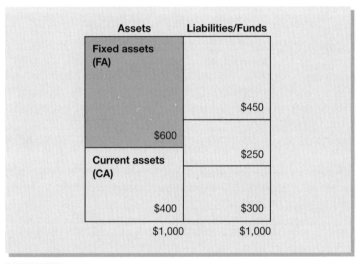

Figure 2.3   The balance sheet – the fixed assets box

We use the term 'fixed assets' even though the block contains items that do not strictly fall under this heading. A more accurate description would be 'long-term investments', but the term 'fixed assets' is more commonly used. Another common description used mainly by large global companies is 'non-current' assets.

The items that fall into this block are grouped under three headings:

1 Intangibles

Included under this heading are all assets that do not have a physical presence. The main item is goodwill. This is a component that gives rise to some controversy although it is outside the scope of this book.

2 Net fixed assets

Large, expensive, long-lasting, physical items required in the operations of the business are included here. Land, buildings, machinery, and office and transport equipment are the common entries. The standard method of valuation is to take original cost and deduct accumulated depreciation. In the case of property, adjustments may be made to reflect current values.

3 Investments

'Investments/other assets' include long-term holdings of shares in other companies for trading purposes. Not all such investments are shown in this way. Where a holding company has dominant influence, the accounts of the subsidiary company are totally consolidated. This means that the separate assets and liabilities of the subsidiary are aggregated with corresponding items in the parent company's balance sheet. It is only investments in non-consolidated companies that are shown here.

The question as to whether the balance sheet values should be adjusted to reflect current market values has, for years, been a contentious one. In times of high inflation, property values get out of line – often considerably so – and it is recommended that they be revalued. However, it is important to note that the balance sheet does not attempt to reflect the market value of either the separate assets or the total company. Prospective buyers or sellers of course examine these matters closely.

Liabilities

The liabilities column is subdivided into the following three categories:

- owners' funds (OF)
- long-term loans (LTL)
- current liabilities (CL).

(There are certain types of funds that do not fit comfortably into any one of the above listed classes. At this stage we will ignore them. Usually the amounts are insignificant.)

Current liabilities (CL)

Current liabilities (see Figure 2.4) have a strong parallel relationship with current assets. For example 'accounts payable' counterbalance 'accounts receivable'. Also 'cash' and 'short-term loans' reflect the day-to-day operating cash position at different stages. We will return to the relationship between current assets and current liabilities later.

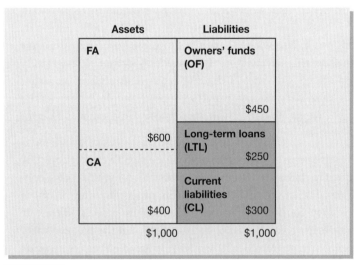

Figure 2.4 The balance sheet - long-term loans and current liabilities

Long-term loans (LTL)

These include mortgages, debentures, term loans, bonds, and any form of debt that has repayment terms longer than one year.

Another common description for long-term loans used mainly by large global companies is 'non-current' liabilities.

Owners' funds (OF)

Owners' funds are the most exciting section of the balance sheet. Included here are all claims by the owners on the business. Here is where fortunes are made and lost. It is where entrepreneurs can exercise their greatest skills and where takeover battles are fought to the finish. Likewise it is the place where 'financial engineers' regularly come up with new schemes designed to bring ever-increasing returns to the brave. Unfortunately, it is also the area where most confusing entries appear in the balance sheet.

In place of the term 'owners' funds' you may find the following alternatives in practice (which largely mean the same thing):

■ owners' funds
■ ordinary funds
■ shareholders' funds
■ total equity.

For the newcomer to the subject the most important thing to remember is that the total in the box is the figure that matters, not the breakdown between many different entries. We will discuss this section at length in Chapter 11 on investor ratios. It is important to note that while our discussions centre on publicly quoted companies, everything said applies equally strongly to non-quoted companies. The rules of the game are the same for both.

Note the three major subdivisions of owners' funds below:

■ issued common stock
■ capital reserves
■ revenue reserves.

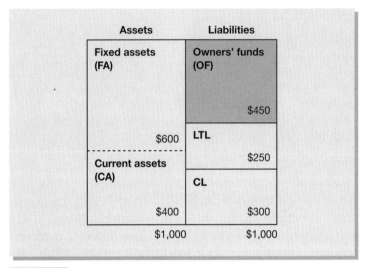

Figure 2.5   The balance sheet – owners' funds

1 Issued common stock

The issuing of common stock for a cash consideration is the main mechanism for bringing owners' capital into the business. Three different values are associated with issued common stock:

- nominal value
- book value
- market value.

These will be covered in detail in Chapter 11 on investor ratios.

2 Capital reserves

The heading 'capital reserves' is used to cover all surpluses accruing to the common stockholders that have not arisen from trading. The main sources of such funds are:

- revaluation of fixed assets
- premiums on shares issued at a price in excess of nominal value
- currency gains on balance sheet items and some non-trading profits.

A significant feature of these reserves is that they cannot easily be paid out as dividends. In many countries there are also statutory reserves where companies are obliged by law to set aside a certain portion of trading profit for specified purposes – generally to do with the health of the firm. These are also treated as capital reserves.

3 Revenue reserves

These are amounts retained in the company from normal trading profit. Many different terms, names, descriptions can be attached to them. Here are the most common:

- revenue reserves
- general reserve
- retained earnings.

This breakdown of revenue reserves into separate categories is unimportant and the terms used are also unimportant. All the above items belong to the common stockholders. They have all come from the same source and they can be distributed as dividends to the shareholders at the will of the directors.

Key balance sheet terms

The following four key terms used in the balance sheet are very simple but important:

- total assets
- capital employed
- net worth
- working capital.

In any discussion of company affairs, these terms turn up again and again, under many different guises and often with different names. Each of these terms will be defined and illustrated in turn. The five-box balance sheet layout will assist us greatly in this section.

Total assets (TA)

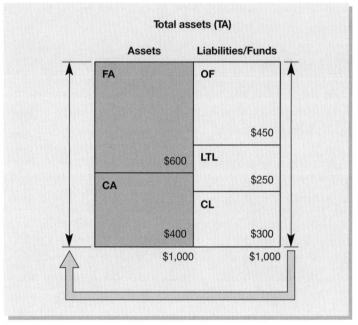

Figure 2.6   Defining total assets

You will see from Figure 2.6 that the definition is straightforward:

TA = FA + CA
$1,000 = $600 + $400

However, very often we use the term 'total assets' when we are really more interested in the right-hand side of the balance sheet where the definition more properly is:

TA = OF + LTL + CL
$1,000 = $450 + $250 + $300

We must be able to see in our mind's eye the relationship that exists between this and other balance sheet definitions.

'Total assets' is a value we will use often. As can be seen, it is simply the sum of everything in the balance sheet from top to bottom. This is the same number whether we use the right-hand or left-hand side.

Sometimes it will make more sense to look at this value from the point of view of the assets and sometimes from the point of view of the funds.

We may use the same expression 'total assets' in both situations.

Please note that sometimes we come across the term 'total tangible assets' in addition to 'total assets'.

 Capital employed (CE)

This is the second important balance sheet term and it is one that is used very widely. Most books on finance give the definition of capital employed as being:

Fixed assets + investments + inventory + accounts receivable + cash, less accounts payable and short-term loans.

To disentangle this definition, look at Figure 2.7 and you will see that it means:

CE = FA + CA — CL
$700 = $600 + $400 — $300

From Figure 2.7, we can see that it also comprises the two upper right-hand boxes of the balance sheet, which gives the definition:

CE = OF + LTL
$700 = $450 + $250

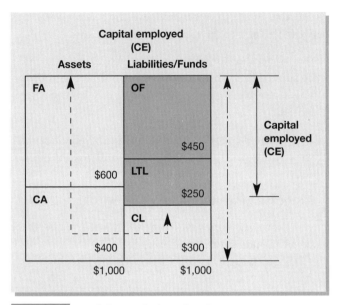

Figure 2.7   Defining capital employed

These definitions are identical.

In the first case, we start off at the top left-hand side, work down through fixed assets and current assets to the very bottom and then come back up through current liabilities to end up at the long-term loans line.

In the second case, we start at the top right-hand side and work our way down through owners' funds and long-term loans.

Either way, we can see that the distinction between total assets and capital employed is that all the *short-term liabilities* in the current liabilities box are deducted from capital employed. Capital employed, therefore, includes only the *long-term funds* sections the balance sheet.

Capital employed is a widely used term. We will often see a rate of return expressed as a percentage of this value. Many analysts place great emphasis on capital employed. They say, with justification, that it represents the long-term foundation funds of the company. In looking at company performance they are concerned to ensure that profits are sufficient to keep this foundation intact. However, others will argue that in the current liabilities category we have, normally, bank borrowings that are, in theory, very short-term but are, in reality, permanent funds. They should therefore be included in the funding base when calculating rates of return.

Net worth (NW)

This third term includes the top right-hand box only of the balance sheet. This box is such a significant section of the balance sheet that it has many names attached to it.

We have already looked at this box in some detail under the heading 'owners' funds'. An alternative name for 'owners' funds' is 'net worth'. As a reminder the following values are included here:

- issued common stock
- capital reserves
- revenue reserves.

Accordingly, the first definition of net worth is the sum of the above three items, amounting to $450 (see Figure 2.8).

For the second definition we can use the same method that we used for capital employed. That is, we work our way down through the assets and back up through the liabilities to arrive at the same value:

$$NW = FA + CA - CL - LTL$$
$$\$450 = \$600 + \$400 - \$300 - \$250$$

This latter definition conveys more accurately the significance of the value in this box. It says to us that the value attributable to the owners in a company is determined by the value of all the assets

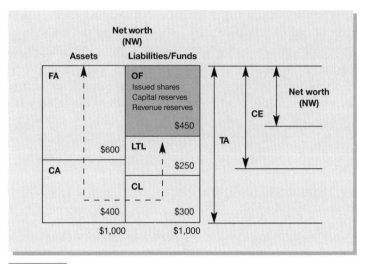

Figure 2.8   Defining net worth

less all external liabilities, both short and long. This is simple common sense. The shareholders' stake in the company is simply the sum of the assets less loans outstanding to third parties. In a set of published accounts this is commonly referred to as 'net assets'.

The first way of looking at this box is by means of the accounting definition, where shares are issued and reserves are accumulated over time using various accounting rules and conventions. The second definition gives a more pragmatic approach: simply take all the values on the assets side of the balance sheet and deduct outstanding loans – anything left is shareholders' money, no matter what name we give it. If recorded book values for assets are close to actual values, both approaches will give almost the same answer.

The amount of realism in the net worth figure, then, depends entirely on the validity of the asset values.

Working capital (WC)

Our fourth balance sheet term is illustrated in Figure 2.9. It is an important term that we will come back to again and again in our business ratios.

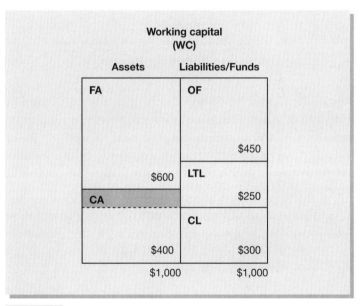

Figure 2.9 Defining working capital

The widely used definition of working capital is:

WC = CA — CL
$100 = $400 — $300

Working capital is an important value. It represents the amount of day-to-day operating liquidity available to a business. We can consider liquidity as an indicator of cash availability. It is clearly not the same thing as wealth: many people and companies who are

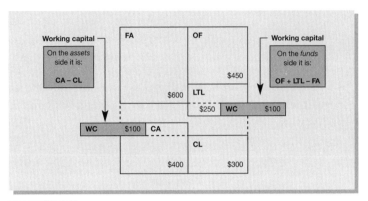

Figure 2.10   Alternative definition of working capital

very wealthy do not have a high degree of liquidity. This happens if the wealth is tied up in assets that are not easily converted into cash. For instance, large farm and plantation owners have lots of assets, but may have difficulty in meeting day-to-day cash demands – they have much wealth but they are not liquid. This can be true for companies also.

It is not sufficient to have assets; it is necessary to ensure that there is sufficient liquidity to meet ongoing cash needs. A company can be very rich in assets, but short of liquidity if these assets cannot readily be converted into cash.

We have an alternative definition in Figure 2.10, that looks at working capital from the right-hand side of the balance sheet. This definition gives perhaps a more significant insight. Here, we see that it can be calculated as:

WC = OF + LTL — FA
$100 = $450 + $250 — $600

This definition is not often used in the literature but it is a very important way of looking at the structure of a company.

The amount of working capital available to a company is determined by the long-term funds that are not tied up in long-term assets. When a business is being set up, long-term funds are injected from the owners and other long sources. A considerable amount of these will be spent to acquire fixed long-term assets. However a sufficient amount must remain to take care of short-term day-to-day working capital requirements. Normally as time goes on this need grows with the development of the company. This need can be met only from additional long-term funds, e.g. retained earnings, or long loans, or from the disposal of fixed assets.

3

The profit and loss account

This chapter will show you:

- How we recognise revenue and costs
- The distinction between profit and cash flow

Introduction

Figure 3.1 identifies where the profit and loss account fits into the set of accounts. It is a link or bridge between the opening and closing balance sheets of an accounting period. Its function is to identify the total revenue earned and the total costs incurred over that period. The difference between these two values is the operating profit. It is, therefore, a document that relates to a very precise time period. There are many accounting rules to do with the identification of revenue and costs.

Revenue

Total revenue earned is generally the amount invoiced and, in most situations, there is no problem with its accurate identification.

'Revenue recognition', the question of when we should recognise revenue in accounts, continues to be a topical accounting issue. Here are three examples of areas of debate:

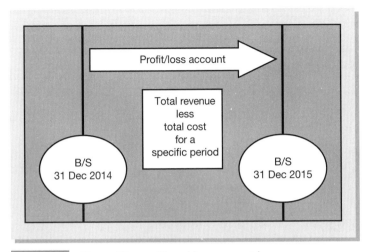

Figure 3.1 Place of the profit and loss account in company

1 If a company receives cash today for a contract to supply a service over three years, should they recognise the revenue now or divide it across the three years?

2 What constitutes revenue in the second year of a large, three-year civil works project?

3 If an engineering company sells a warehouse, is that part of revenue?

Costs

The figure for total costs can give rise to even more intractable problems.

Two rules will help to identify costs that must be included:

■ those costs that relate directly to the revenue, for example the direct cost of the goods sold; and

■ those costs that relate to the time period covered by the accounts, such as staff salaries for the period.

Even with these rules, however, there are still many areas where the decision could go either way. For example, should research and development costs be charged in the year in which they were incurred? If we replace the factory roof in a period, is that correctly chargeable as a cost? We could question whether a particular depreciation charge is correct. The list can go on.

In the analysis of a company's accounts, it is well to ask what important assumptions or accounting policies have had an effect on the final profit.

In all published accounts there should be a statement of accounting policies. It is wise to examine it before attempting an analysis of the financial statements.

Common causes of confusion

In a situation where accountants can sometimes differ, it is not surprising that non-accounting managers go astray. One or two basic signposts will eliminate many problems that arise for the non-specialist in understanding this account.

The distinction between profit and cash flow is a common cause of confusion. The profit and loss account as such is not concerned with cash flow. This is covered by a separate statement. For instance, a cost from a supplier incurred but not yet paid must be charged as cost even though there has been no cash flow. On the other hand, payments to suppliers for goods received are not costs, simply cash flow. Costs are incurred when goods are consumed, not when they are purchased or paid for.

Cash spent on the purchase of assets is not a cost. The cost recognised is the corresponding depreciation over the following years.

A loan repayment is not a cost because an asset (cash) and a liability (loan) are both reduced by the same amount, so there is no loss in value by this transaction.

Finally the question of timing is vital. Having established what the true costs and revenue are, we must locate them in the correct time period. The issue mainly arises just before and just after the cut-off date between accounting periods. As shown in Figure 3.2,

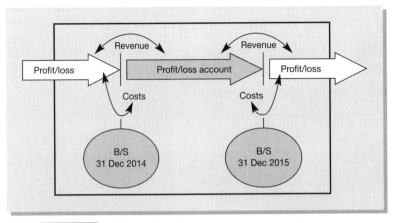

Figure 3.2 The profit and loss account – timing adjustments

we may have to move revenue or costs forwards or backwards to get them into their correct time periods.

Alternative measures of profit

There are many other definitions of profit, mostly related to the way profit is distributed. In many businesses the term 'bottom line' is commonly used. Each of the following measures could be used as suitable alternative 'bottom lines'.

 ## EBIT (Earnings before interest and tax)

This is the first profit figure we encounter in the profit and loss account. It is also known as PBIT (profit before interest and tax) or alternatively operating profit or even trading profit.

In simple terms it is just total revenue less total operating cost.

All the business's assets have played a part in generating operating profit or EBIT. Therefore this profit belongs to and must be distributed among those who have provided the assets. This is done according to well defined rules.

Figure 3.3 illustrates the process of distribution or 'appropriation' of profit. There is a fixed order in the queue for distribution as follows:

- to the lenders (interest)
- to the taxation authorities (tax)
- to the shareholders (dividends/retentions).

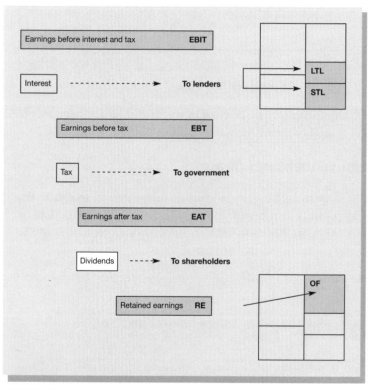

Figure 3.3 The profit and loss account – distribution or appropriation of profits

The profit and loss appropriation account

At each of the stages of appropriation the profit remaining is given a precise identification tag. Stripped of non-essentials, the following is a layout of a standard profit and loss appropriation account. When looking at a set of accounts for the first time it may be difficult to see this structure because the form of layout is not as regular as we see in the balance sheet. However, if one starts at the EBT figure, it is usually possible to work up and down to the other items shown:

	$
EBIT (Earnings before interest and tax)	X
– Less interest	(X)
EBT (Earnings before tax)	X
– Less tax	(X)
EAT (Earnings after tax)	X
– Less dividends	(X)
RE (Retained earnings)	X

EBT (Earnings before tax)

This is the profit remaining after debt providers have been paid. It is a commonly used performance measure for divisions of a large business, where tax is organised and paid centrally.

EBT is sometimes referred to as PBT (profit before tax).

EAT (Earnings after tax)

This is the profit remaining after both debt providers and the tax authorities have been paid.

EAT is used to calculate distributable profits (usually the same as EAT but there are exceptions), which is the profit left for the shareholders out of which dividends can be paid.

EAT is sometimes referred to as PAT (profit after tax).

We will return to EAT when we review investor ratios in Chapter 11, as it is used to calculate the important ratio of earnings per share (EPS).

 ## RE (Retained earnings)

This is the profit left in the business after debt providers, tax authorities and shareholders have been paid.

Retained earnings are an important source of business finance. If earnings are retained within a business it can be a sign that the directors are confident about the future. The business could be 'saving' for a future investment opportunity. Retained earnings also increase the owners' funds section of the balance sheet, which in turn will increase the value of the business. The size of owners' funds also impacts on 'leverage', covered in Chapter 9 on financial strength.

part

two

Operating performance

4

The big picture

This chapter will:

- Look at the balance sheet and profit and loss account together
- Introduce you to an example company with some example data
- Cover two alternative balance sheet layouts

Working data

Throughout the various stages of the book we will work with an illustrative set of data for an example company.

The Example Co. plc

Figure 4.1 shows for the Example Co. plc:

- the balance sheet
- the profit and loss account
- share data.

The Example Co. plc has been devised with simple numbers to highlight various aspects of accounts and show the calculation of ratios.

Example Co. plc

Balance sheet

$m

Fixed assets	$	$	Owners' funds	$	$
Intangibles	0		Issued capital	80	
Net fixed assets	440		Capital reserves	60	
Investments	40		Revenue reserves	220	
					360
		480	**Long-term loans**		
					200
Current assets					
Inventory	128		**Current liabilities**		
Accounts receivable	160		Short-term loans	60	
Cash	20		Accounts payable	140	
Miscellaneous	12		Miscellaneous	40	
		320			240
		800			800

Profit and loss account

$m

		$	$
Sales			1,120
Operating costs			1,008
EBIT (Earnings before interest and tax)			112
	Interest	20	
EBT (Earnings before tax)			92
	Tax	32	
EAT (Earnings after tax)			60
	Dividends	24	
RE (Retained earnings)			36

Share data

Number of ordinary shares	= 32,000,000
Share market price	= $22.5

Figure 4.1   Working data – the Example Co. plc

It is worthwhile spending a moment looking over the now familiar five-box balance sheet and the structured profit and loss account to become familiar with the figures. They will be used a lot in the following chapters.

Balance sheet layouts

A number of alternative forms of layout, particularly in the case of the balance sheet, are used in presenting accounts. While the layout itself does not affect any of the numbers, it can be difficult when faced with an unfamiliar format to find where items are located and to calculate values for key ratios such as 'total assets' and 'capital employed'.

The first point to remember is that the items within each of the five boxes will always appear grouped together – they are never scattered around among other items. Sometimes, however, the total only of a subsection will appear in the balance sheet while the detail is to be found in the notes to accounts.

Vertical balance sheet – version 1

Given the five-box grouping, it follows that there is only a limited number of ways in which the boxes can be arranged. In Figure 4.2, one such re-arrangement is shown.

It is easy to see how the items in the two-column format have been re-ordered into a single vertical column. This type of layout has the advantage that corresponding values for successive years can be laid out side by side for ease of comparison. In this format, values for 'total assets' and 'total funds' are also emphasised.

Note that the order of the boxes may be different depending on the accounting jurisdiction and convention. For example, current assets may be shown before long-term assets, and similarly in respect to liabilities.

Vertical balance sheet – version 2

The second layout, as shown in Figure 4.3, is a slightly more sophisticated version and is often seen in published accounts. The difference is that current liabilities have been moved out of the liabilities section and are instead shown as a negative value side by side with current assets. The totals of these two sections are netted off to give the figure for 'working capital'.

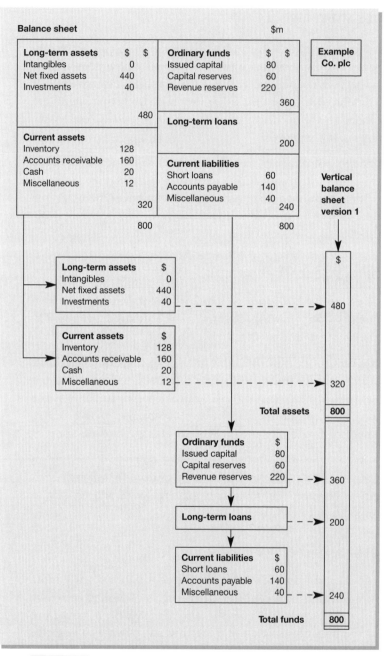

Figure 4.2 Vertical sheet version 1 using data from the Example Co. plc

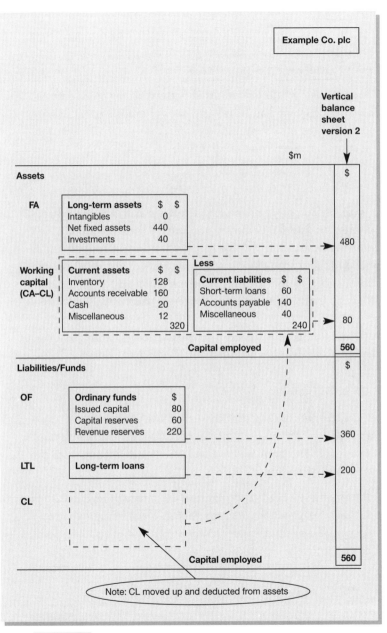

Figure 4.3 Vertical sheet version 2 using data from the Example Co. plc

Both sides of the balance sheet are, accordingly, reduced by the amount of the current liabilities – $240. The original totals amounted to $800, so the new balancing figure is $560. This figure, as seen earlier, is 'capital employed'.

The advantage of this layout is that both working capital (current assets less current liabilities) and capital employed values are identified. The disadvantage is that the figure for total assets does not appear anywhere on the balance sheet.

Which format?

It is largely a matter of personal preference as to which format is adopted for internal company accounts. For external published company accounts it is down to jurisdiction and convention as well as local company law. In the three types of layouts illustrated (the five-box format and vertical versions 1 and 2), practically all possible situations have been covered, so most balance sheets should now make sense. It is a good idea to take whatever form is used and transfer the figures into the familiar five-box format as the significant features will then quickly become evident.

A note on terminology

As mentioned earlier the heading 'Non-current assets and liabilities' is often used in place of 'Long-term assets and liabilities'. In this book we have used the heading 'Long-term' for ease of understanding.

Additionally, the headings 'Creditors: amounts falling due within one year' and 'Creditors: amounts falling due after more than one year' can also be used to refer to current liabilities and long-term loans respectively.

5

Return on investment

This chapter will:

- Review the term 'return on investment'
- Explore its various derivative measures

The generic term 'return on investment' is one of the most important concepts in business finance.

Every dollar of assets can be matched to a dollar of funds provided by the financial markets. The providers of these funds need to be paid. Payment comes from the operating surplus (or profit) generated from the utilisation of assets. Return on investment measures operating surplus as a proportion of the underlying assets/funds required to generate that surplus.

If return on investment is equal to or greater than the cost of funds, then the business is viable. However, if return on investment (in the long term) is less than the cost of funds, the business has no future.

The concept of return on investment is universal, but the methods of measurement vary widely. This lack of consistency causes confusion in the minds of many financial and non-financial people alike. This chapter aims to clear this confusion.

When we wish to examine a company's performance, we look at its absolute profit (from the profit/loss account) in relation to the assets tied up in the business (from the balance sheet). But the question arises: which figure should we take from the profit/loss account, and which figure from the balance sheet?

Figure 5.1 shows the accounts for the Example Co. plc with values extracted for:

Profit and loss account
- EBIT
- EBT
- EAT

Balance sheet
- TA
- CE
- NW

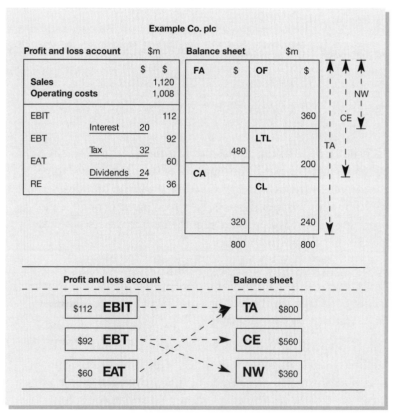

Figure 5.1   Important terms from the profit and loss account and balance sheet using data from the Example Co. plc

Performance is measured by establishing relationships between these two sets of values.

However, we have a choice as to which value we use from each statement. Earnings before interest and tax could be measured against total assets or capital employed or net worth. We could do likewise with earnings before tax and earnings after tax. This gives us nine possible measures of performance. In practice, we meet with all of these measures and even with some other variations.

Various names are given to these linkages or ratios between the balance sheet and the profit and loss account values. In practice almost all combinations are used. Their respective popularity changes according to the latest trend.

The names come and go, becoming popular for a while and then maybe disappearing. A selection of these measures are:

- ROA (return on assets)
- ROTA (return on total assets)
- RONA (return on net assets)
- ROCE (return on capital employed)
- ROIC (return of invested capital)
- ROE (return on equity).

This multiplicity of terms causes difficulty to the non-specialist, but the point to remember is that these are not different ratios. They all simply measure in one way or another the return on investment. The name used does not greatly matter. What is important, however, is that we know which profit and loss figure is being related to which balance sheet figure.

This book will initially use only two measures of return on investment:

- ROTA (return on total assets)
- ROE (return on equity).

ROTA gives a measure of the operating efficiency of the total business.

ROE assesses the return made to the equity shareholder.

Each will be covered in detail below.

We do not imply that these are the only correct measures or that all others are deficient in some way. However, they are two of the better measures. There is sound logic for choosing them in preference to others, as we will see in due course.

These two separate measures are necessary because they throw light on different aspects of the business, both of which are important.

Return on total assets looks at the operating efficiency of the total enterprise, while return on equity considers how that operating efficiency is translated into benefit to the owners.

 ## Return on equity (ROE)

This ratio is arguably the most important in business finance. It measures the absolute return delivered to the shareholders. A good figure brings success to the business – it results in a high share price and makes it easy to attract new funds. This will enable the company to grow, given suitable market conditions, and leads to greater profits. In turn, this leads to high value and the continued growth in wealth of its owners.

At the individual business level, a good return on equity will keep in place the financial framework for a thriving, growing enterprise. At the total economy level, return on equity drives positive contributions such as:

- industrial investment
- growth in gross national product
- employment
- government tax receipts.

It is, therefore, a critical feature of the overall modern market economy as well as of individual companies.

Figure 5.2 shows how return on equity is calculated. The figure for EAT from the profit and loss account is expressed as a percentage of OF (owners' funds/net worth) from the balance sheet.

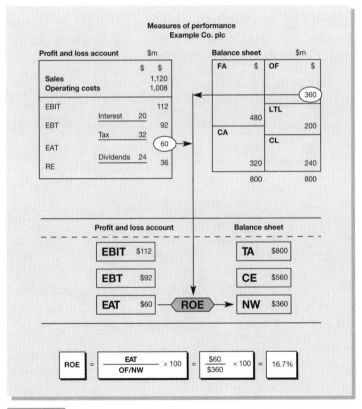

Figure 5.2   Return on equity ratio applied to data from the Example Co. plc

Return on total assets (ROTA)

Return on total assets provides the foundation necessary for a company to deliver a good return on equity. ROTA is the most important driver of ROE. A company without a good ROTA finds it almost impossible to generate a satisfactory ROE.

Figure 5.3 shows how ROTA is calculated. The figure for EBIT (or operating profit) from the profit and loss account is expressed as a percentage of total assets from the balance sheet.

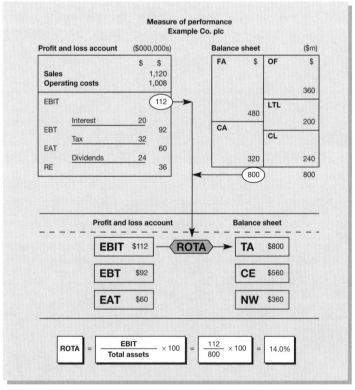

Figure 5.3   Return on total assets ratio applied to data from the Example Co. plc

ROTA calculates a rate of return earned on assets and therefore measures how well management utilises the business's assets to generate an operating surplus.

Some practitioners contend that the figure taken from the balance sheet should include the long-term funds and only those short-term funds for which a charge is made, i.e. STL (short-term loans). Their position is that assets funded by 'free' creditors should not be included in the rate of return calculation. There is considerable merit in this argument, but a potentially stronger counter-argument is that the rate of return issue is separate from the funding issue and that assets should produce a return irrespective of the method of funding. For example, some companies choose to fund by suppliers' credit, others from a bank loan.

Whichever method of calculation is adopted, return on total assets uses the three main operating variables of the business:

- total revenue
- total cost
- assets utilised.

ROTA is therefore the most comprehensive measure of total management performance available to us.

Alternative return on investment measures

There are many other possible variations of 'return on investment'. Some may well be more suitable for particular types of businesses. One that is widely used is ROCE (return on capital employed).

As covered in Chapter 2, capital employed is calculated as total assets less current liabilities. The corresponding profit and loss value used is EBIT. Because a smaller denominator is used in calculating return on capital employed, we would expect a higher answer than for return on total assets.

When new expressions for these ratios are encountered it is often not clear which profit and loss value is being measured against which balance sheet value. Then the question to ask is 'How is it calculated?' When you know what the calculation method is, it is as easy to work with one combination as another. However, there is a certain logic that should be followed in deciding on any particular ratio – if the value from the balance sheet includes loans, then the profit and loss value should include the corresponding interest charge and vice versa. This rule is not always adhered to and the resulting answers can be suspect.

6

Performance drivers

The chapter reviews the drivers of:

- Return on investment
- Profit margin
- Asset turnover

The key drivers of ROTA

ROTA is a key tool in directing management's day-to-day activities. It provides a benchmark against which all operations can be measured. However, as a single figure it simply provides a target. To be useful in decision-making it must first be broken down into its component parts.

We will do this in two stages.

- First, we will divide the main ROTA ratio into two subsidiary ratios.
- Then we will divide the subsidiary ratios into further detailed constituents.

ROTA is calculated as:

$$\frac{\text{EBIT}}{\text{TA}}$$

We can relate 'sales' to both EBIT and TA to produce two subsidiary ratios:

1. Profit margin (or margin on sales)

$$\frac{\text{EBIT}}{\text{Sales}}$$

Profit margin identifies profit as a percentage of sales and is often described as the net profit margin. It is a well-known measure and almost universally used in the monitoring of a company's profitability.

 ## 2. Asset turnover

$$\frac{\text{Sales}}{\text{TA}}$$

Asset turnover looks at the total sales achieved by the company in relation to its total assets. This measure is often less emphasised in the assessment of company performance. However its contribution to ROTA is just as powerful and important as the profit margin.

It is simple mathematics to show that the product of these will always combine to the value of ROTA.

This first split is so important that we will take the risk of over-emphasising it here. The formula is:

ROTA   =   Profit margin   ×   Asset turnover

$$\frac{\text{EBIT}}{\text{TA}} \quad = \quad \frac{\text{EBIT}}{\text{Sales}} \quad × \quad \frac{\text{Sales}}{\text{TA}}$$

$$\frac{112}{800} \quad = \quad \frac{112}{1,120} \quad × \quad \frac{1,120}{800}$$

14%   =   10%   ×   1.4 times

This uses numbers from Example Co. plc.

The importance of this interrelationship of ratios is difficult to exaggerate. To repeat our logic so far:

■ ROE is the most important driver of company value
■ ROTA is the most important driver of ROE.

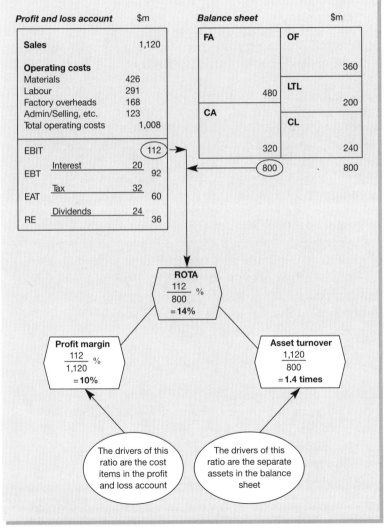

Figure 6.1   Profit margin and asset turnover ratios applied to data from the Example Co. plc

Therefore, the ratios that drive ROTA are:

- Profit margin (margin on sales percentage)
- Asset turnover (sales to total assets ratio).

Illustration of the interrelationship between profit margin and asset turnover

Figure 6.2 shows some typical values for companies with vastly different profiles (using illustrative numbers).

Example A

Example A shows typical figures for a distribution-type company, where low margins, e.g. 5 to 7%, combine with a high asset turnover, e.g. 2 times.

Example B

In Example B the opposite applies. Very high margins and low asset turnover are typical of companies that require large quantities of fixed assets. The telecommunications sector typically generates sales margins in the region of 25%. However, their enormous investment in fixed assets with correspondingly low asset turnover means that this margin is only just adequate to make a reasonable return on total assets.

Example C

Example C demonstrates fairly average figures, with margins at 10% or more, and asset turnover values somewhat greater than 1. Quite a number of medium-sized manufacturing companies have this kind of pattern. The difference between success and mediocrity in this type of business is often less than 2% on margin and a small improvement in asset turnover.

It rests with the skill of each management team to discover for itself the unique combination of margin and asset turnover that will give their company its own particular, and successful, market niche.

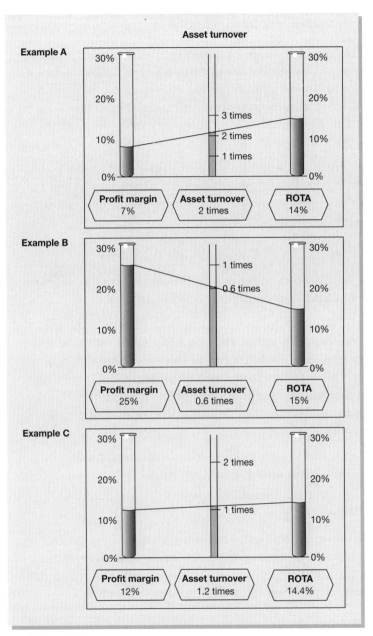

Figure 6.2   Indicative profit margin and asset turnover
ratios for different types of business

Drivers of operating performance

ROTA typically averages around 12.5% (plus or minus 5%) across industries. Please recognise that this is an average and there will be a wide spread of results within every industry. Whereas it is possible to see an average across industries, the subsidiary ratios of profit margin and asset turnover vary widely across different sectors.

A rule of thumb would be that a profit margin of approximately 10%, combined with an asset turnover of between 1.3 and 1.5, would be where many Western companies would find a comfortable and profitable position.

The key drivers of profit margin and asset turnover

We have now derived two most important ratios that drive return on total assets, 'profit margin' and 'asset turnover'.

It is on these two drivers that managers must concentrate in order to improve performance. However, these ratios cannot be operated on directly. Each is dependent on a whole series of detailed results from widely separated parts of the operation. These in turn can be expressed in ratio form and all that managers need is a system that will enable them to identify and quantify these subsidiary values so that they can:

- set the target value for each ratio that, if achieved, will deliver the required overall performance level
- delegate the achievement of these targets to specific individuals.

The system outlined in the following pages achieves this end. It will be seen that it incorporates all the main elements in both the profit and loss account and balance sheet. Each of the elements is a performance driver and must be managed accordingly.

Drivers of profit margin

The drivers of profit margin (or margin on sales) are the cost items in the profit and loss account.

At its simplest, we can say that the margin is what is left when the total operating cost is deducted.

If the margin were 10%, the total cost would be 90%. The margin can be improved only if this 90% can be reduced. To reduce the figure, we must know its component parts. So, the next stage is to identify the separate cost elements and see what percentage each of the main cost elements bears to sales (see Figure 6.3).

Figure 6.3 shows the development of the left-hand side of the model, which is concerned with profit and loss values. The four main cost elements that accumulate to total operating costs are identified as materials, labour, factory overheads and admin/ selling. These large cost groups are used as an example: in practice they would be broken down into much more detail.

In the bottom half of the diagram, each cost element is shown expressed as a percentage of sales. For instance, the first box shows that materials is 38% (material cost of $426 over sales of $1,120 multiplied by 100). The sum total of all the costs is 90%, giving a margin of 10%.

If management wishes to improve this margin, then one or more of the cost percentages must fall. For instance, if the material cost percentage could be reduced by two points, from 38 to 36%, then, other things being equal, the margin percentage would improve by two points to 12%. This margin of 12% would then combine with the sales to total assets ratio of 1.4 times to give an improved return on total assets of 16.8% (that is, 12% multiplied by 1.4).

These cost ratios allow managers to plan, budget, delegate responsibility and monitor the performance of the various functional areas under their control. They can quantify targets for all areas, and calculate the effect of a variation in any one of the subsidiary ratios on the overall performance.

The results achieved by different managers, products and divisions can also be compared and the experiences of the best passed on to the others to help them improve. We must recognise,

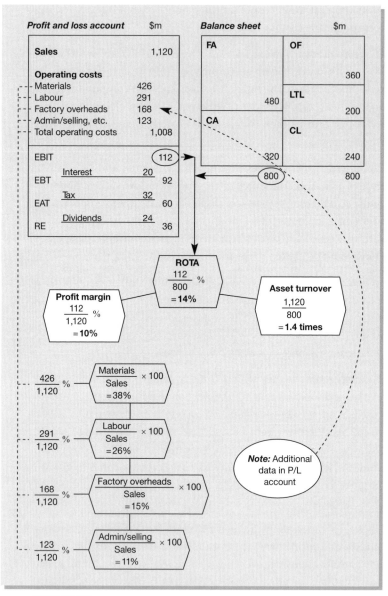

Figure 6.3   Drivers of profit margin applied to data from the Example Co. plc

however, that there are operating factors that the model does not cope with. The variables of selling price, volume and product mix, which have such a powerful impact on profit, are not easily distinguished from other factors in the model.

Drivers of asset turnover

The drivers of asset turnover (or the sales to total assets ratio) are the separate assets in the balance sheet.

Asset turnover can also be broken down into its component parts. We identify the main groups of assets straight from the balance sheet and we then express the ratio between each group and the sales figure as shown in Figure 6.4.

In Figure 6.4 it will be seen that just as the subsidiary values of the left-hand side were derived from the profit and loss account, so these right-hand elements are taken from the balance sheet. Each of the main asset categories is related to sales.

The three major asset blocks in most enterprises are:

▪ fixed assets
▪ inventories (stocks)
▪ accounts receivable (debtors).

The value of each in relation to sales is shown in the subsidiary boxes. For instance, the ratio for fixed assets is 2.5 times (from sales of $1,120 divided by fixed assets of $440). Note that the sum of these separate values does not agree with the sales to total assets ratio as did the sales margin on the other side with the operating costs. This is because they are expressed differently. If the reciprocals of the values are taken, the link will become clear.

To managers, this display shows the importance of managing the balance sheet as well as the profit and loss account. For instance, if the total assets could be reduced from $800 to $700, through stronger credit control, for example, then the sales to total assets ratio would move up from 1.4 to 1.6 times. The effect on the return on total assets would be to increase it from 14% to 16%. If,

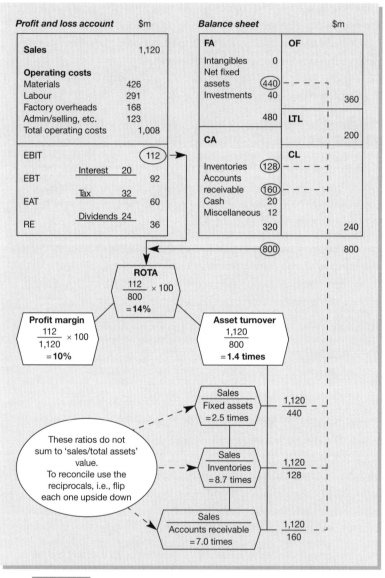

Figure 6.4 Drivers of asset turnover ratio applied to data from the Example Co. plc

in addition, the profit margin was increased by 1% to 11%, then the new return on total assets would be almost 18% (11% × 1.6). The original value of 14% for ROTA is an average value whereas a return on total assets of 18% represents an excellent performance.

In these areas, production managers can work with finance and marketing departments to quantify targets for stock holdings and accounts receivable. The impact of an increase in fixed assets caused by a major capital investment project can also be assessed in profitability terms.

The complete operating profit model

The complete model is shown in Figure 6.5. It gives a very powerful insight into the drivers of good performance. It enables managers and functions to work better together as a team. It helps with the definition of responsibilities, delegation of authority and target setting. It provides a powerful framework for a management information system. However, there are a number of issues the model does not highlight.

First, a business normally deals not just in one product, but in a broad range. Cost percentages are averages of the cost elements of the individual products. For management control, it is not satisfactory to work with averages because favourable movements in one product will mask adverse movements in another.

Second, a cost percentage, such as materials, can vary for two totally different reasons:

▪ a change in the absolute material cost per unit
▪ a change in the unit selling price of the product.

The model, however, cannot distinguish between these two causes, despite the fact that one of the most effective ways to reduce the cost percentages is a price increase.

Third, the model does not cope very well with changes in volume, which can be one of the most powerful ways open to

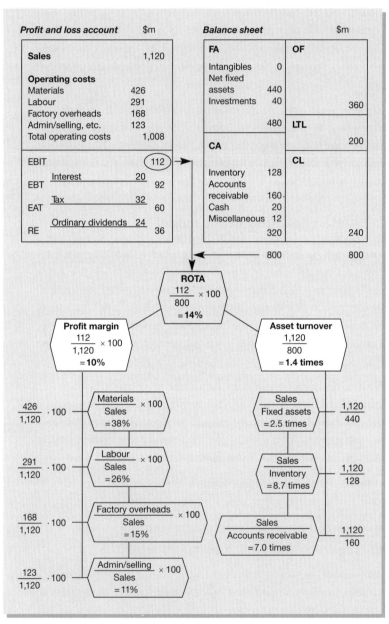

Figure 6.5 Completed operating profit model applied to data from the Example Co. plc

a company to improve performance. A volume increase will certainly be picked up by the sales to total assets ratio – a 10% improvement in volume would move this ratio up from 1.4 to 1.54 times. Additionally, due to fixed costs, the volume change is likely to have an effect on the profit margin as well. When volume increases fixed costs are spread over a larger number of sales units, increasing the profit per unit.

Fourth, those who are perceptive will have noted that this ratio is dependent on the valuation of the assets in the balance sheet. Difficulties can arise when we compare different businesses or divisions because of factors such as the age of plant and different depreciation policies.

Model variations

Many business ratios appear under different names, or are calculated differently, and this can cause some confusion. In the set of ratios we are looking at here, there are two that appear under a number of different guises.

Sales to accounts receivable

This ratio is commonly expressed in terms of days' sales and the method of calculation is shown in Figure 6.6. Instead of the formula we have been using here of sales over accounts receivable, the alternative is to show accounts receivable over sales and multiply the result by 365. The answer represents the average number of days credit customers take before paying off their accounts.

This ratio is often referred to as 'debtor days' or the 'collection period'. The concept of the number of days outstanding is easy to understand. The number is very precise, which means that a slippage of even a few days is instantly identified. Also, figures can be compared with the company's normal terms of trade and the effectiveness or otherwise of the credit control department can, therefore, be monitored.

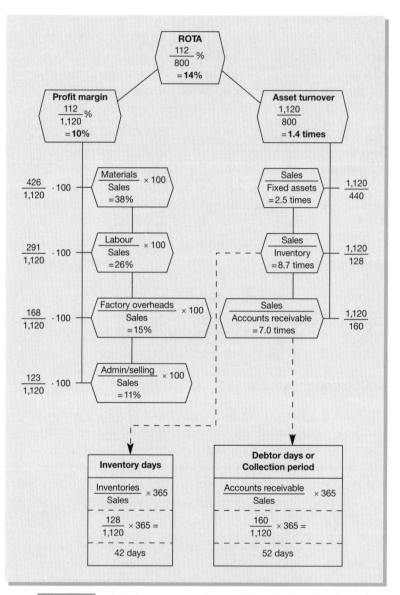

Figure 6.6 Variations to operating model applied to data from the Example Co. plc

This ratio will vary according to local and industry business practice as well as geographical location. Averages in the US and UK are usually around 40 days. Debtor days elsewhere in the EU are typically higher. Japan is known to have low levels of debtor days.

Companies will vary their methods of calculation to reflect their own business circumstances and to provide answers that make sense to them in particular. For instance:

▪ VAT may be included in the debtors but not the sales figure and this distortion will have to be removed.

▪ When there is a heavy seasonal variation, the monthly figures calculated in the normal way may not be very helpful and so the company may work, not on an annual sales basis, but on quarterly sales figures that are annualised.

Sales to inventories

This calculation is similar to the one above and is also known as inventory days or stock days. The link of inventories with sales is not so close as that of sales with accounts receivable. It may, therefore, be linked to purchases or material usage, whichever gives the most useful guidance.

This ratio will vary according to the nature of the industry (for example, manufacturers are likely to hold more inventory than a service business), location and proximity to transport networks and relationships with suppliers.

Corporate liquidity

7

The operating cash cycle

This chapter reviews:

- The concept of corporate liquidity
- The cash cycle
- Matching short-term and long-term liquidity

Corporate liquidity

A company must maintain sufficient cash resources to pay all legitimate bills as they arise. A company that cannot do so has run out of liquidity and is in a very serious financial condition. Ironically, this is so even if it is currently generating good profits.

Cash in this case can be a bank account with a positive balance, or it can be a loan facility that the company has authority to draw down.

When cash runs out, the company's management has lost the power to make independent decisions. An outside agency, such as an unpaid creditor or a bank whose loan is in default, will often decide the fate of the company.

That fate could be insolvency, a forced reconstruction, an involuntary takeover, or the company could be allowed to continue in some altered form. The reality is that management has lost its authority. It is also likely that the owners have lost their entire investment.

One may well ask, 'How can this happen if profits are good?' The answer is that it does happen and for reasons that will become clearer later.

Loss of profits is often the immediate cause of the disaster, but, as we have said, it can happen even when companies are making good profits. Indeed, profitable and rapidly growing small companies very often run out of cash. They then pass out of the hands of the original owner or entrepreneur, who is left with nothing while others reap the benefits of his enterprise.

This chapter will examine corporate liquidity and the factors that drive it. It will look at how we can measure a company's liquid health. It will identify the forces that bring benefit or harm to it.

The cash cycle

The flow of cash through an organisation can be compared with the flow of blood around the body. When we look at the cash flow diagram in Figure 7.1, the reason for this is obvious. Cash is in continuous circulation through the 'arteries' of the business carrying value to its various 'organs'. If this flow is stopped, or even severely reduced for a time, then serious consequences result.

This diagram shows part of the total cash cycle, the part that we refer to as the working capital cash flow. Central to the system is a cash tank, or reservoir, through which cash flows constantly.

It is crucial to the independent survival of the business that this tank does not run dry.

Supporting the cash tank is a supplementary supply, representing unused short-term loan facilities. These provide a first line of defence against a cash shortage. Day-to-day liquidity consists of these two separate cash reservoirs:

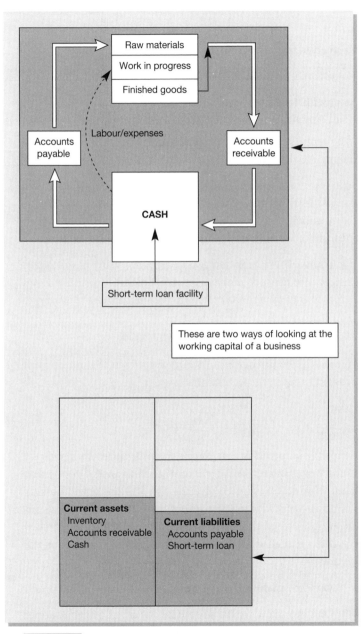

Figure 7.1   The operating cash cycle

The main flow of cash into the reservoir comes from 'accounts receivable'. These are the customers who pay for the goods or services received from the company.

The main cash outflows can be identified under two headings:

- payments to 'accounts payable', that is the suppliers of raw materials and services
- payments of staff salaries/wages, and payments of all other operating expenses.

We can trace the steps in the cycle. 'Accounts payable' supply 'raw materials'. In time these pass through 'work in process' into the 'finished goods' category. During this conversion, cash is absorbed in the form of labour and expenses and payments to suppliers.

In due course, these 'finished goods' are sold. Value passes down the artery into the 'accounts receivable' box, from which it flows back into the 'cash' reservoir to complete the cycle.

Cash flow – the role of profit and depreciation

In Figure 7.2, two further input values are shown that produce an increase in the cash in circulation:

- profit
- depreciation.

The input from profit is easy to understand. Normally goods are sold at a price that exceeds total cost. For instance if goods that cost $100 are sold at a price of $125, the $25 profit will quickly flow into the business in the form of cash. It is a little more difficult to understand the input from 'depreciation'. But depreciation is often quoted as a source of funds and we may have seen the definition:

operating cash flow = operating profit + depreciation

It is not easy to see why this should be. What is so special about depreciation? The answer is that, for most companies, depreciation is the only cost item in the profit and loss account that does

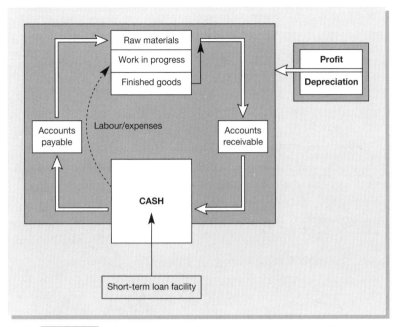

Figure 7.2   The operating cash cycle and the role of profit and depreciation

not have a cash outflow attached to it. Although we just referred to depreciation as a source of cash, it is really the avoidance of a cash outflow. This point is more fully developed in the following section.

It must be emphasised that, even though depreciation does not have a related cash outflow, it is a true cost nevertheless. The relevant cash outflow has simply taken place at an earlier time when the associated fixed asset was purchased. When the fixed asset was purchased, the cash cost was not charged against profits. It was, instead, added to the balance sheet. As the asset is used up, an appropriate amount of cost is released into the profit and loss account. This is what depreciation is all about.

What Figure 7.2 shows is that, with every full cycle, the amount of cash in circulation is increased by the profit earned plus the depreciation charged.

Depreciation and cash flow

The example in Figure 7.3 illustrates the relationship between depreciation and cash flow. This relationship gives rise to much confusion, so we will take the time to explain it here.

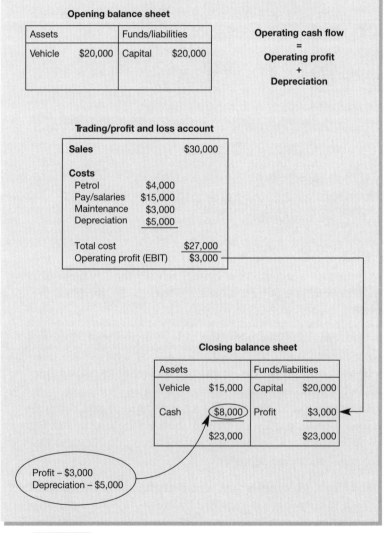

Figure 7.3   The relationship between depreciation and cash flow

Please note that the diagram refers to 'Trading/profit and loss account'. This is because we are simply looking at operating profit (or EBIT) here as opposed to the 'full' profit and loss account.

The example uses the illustration of a very small haulage business. It has one single asset, namely a vehicle valued at $20,000 that the owner uses to transport goods on a job-by-job basis. The business has no inventories or accounts receivable. It has no bank or other loans and all its transactions are carried out for cash.

The opening balance sheet is simple. It shows a single asset of $20,000 that is represented by capital of the same amount.

The profit and loss account highlights are:

- sales of $30,000
- total costs of $27,000
- profit of $3,000.

The closing balance sheet shows a cash figure of $8,000. The company started with no cash and ended up with $8,000, but the profit was only $3,000. How can this be?

We run down through the items of cost and find that the depreciation charge is $5,000. No cash was paid out under this heading. The trading cash receipts were $30,000 and the trading cash costs were $22,000. Therefore the net cash from trading was $8,000. However from this net cash we must deduct depreciation to give the profit of $3,000.

Therefore it is simply a convenient shortcut to arrive at cash flow by adding back depreciation to profit.

An interesting aspect of the depreciation effect is that certain types of companies can suffer serious trading losses without suffering from cash shortages. These are companies where depreciation is a big percentage of total cost, e.g. transportation or utility companies. So long as losses are less than the depreciation charged in the accounts, their operations are cash positive.

Non-operating cash outflows

In Figures 7.1 and 7.2 we saw cash flowing round in a closed circuit. If there were no leaks from this circuit, there would be few problems. However, this is not the case and we must now add further sections to the diagram to allow for cash outflows that are not related to day-to-day operations.

In Figure 7.4 the principal additional outflows are shown as:

- interest, tax and dividends
- loan repayments
- capital expenditure.

We will discuss each in turn.

Interest, tax and dividends

Interest, tax and dividends are deducted from EBIT in the 'profit and loss account'. They represent a distribution of most of the profit earned for the period. Possibly 75% of the profit in any year goes out under these headings, to leave approximately 25% that is permanently retained in the business.

Cash flow should remain positive even after these charges. Furthermore, as regards timing, the profit is usually realised in cash well ahead of these outflows. So this first set of payments should not, of themselves, be a cause of cash embarrassment.

Loan repayments

Loan repayments (as opposed to interest payments on loans) can be substantial in amount. They are also deducted from after-tax income and are in no way connected with the profit for the period. Therefore they can give rise to heavily negative cash positions. However, the amounts required are known well in advance and, in most situations, can be planned and provided for.

Capital expenditure

Capital expenditure is nearly always a matter of policy. It can probably be deferred in unfavourable circumstances. It is

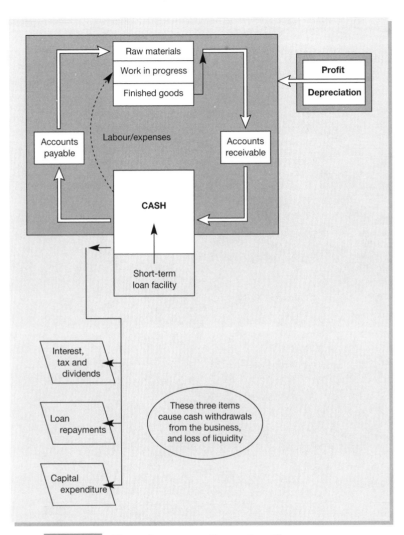

Figure 7.4   The main non-operating cash outflows

subjected to much thought, analysis and planning. Nevertheless heavy expenditure on projects that do not perform to plan is one of the major causes of cash difficulties.

Non-operating cash inflows

In Figure 7.5, the right-hand final branch of the diagram has been completed.

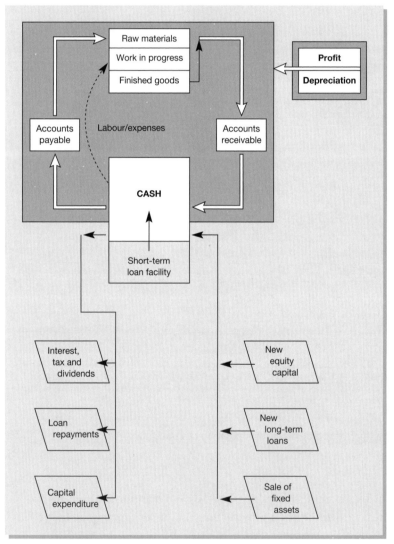

Figure 7.5 The main non-operating cash outflows

Three sources of cash from external sources are shown feeding into the cash reservoir. These are:

- new equity capital
- new long-term loans
- sale of fixed assets.

In many parts of the world a fourth source of cash is available in the form of grants from government to stimulate investment and employment. This has been ignored here for simplicity.

New equity capital and new long-term loans are the two principal sources of long-term finance to a company. In comparing these sources we must give attention to the following three matters:

- cost
- risk
- control.

New equity capital

It is a function of the stock market (or stock exchange) to raise funds for commercial enterprises. A constant stream of public companies go to the stock market to raise cash from the general public or from financial institutions.

The great advantage of equity capital is that it is permanent and it carries no risk to the company. However, it is high-cost money and expensive in terms of control.

New long-term loans

Companies are continually repaying old debts and raising new ones. They must have long-term loan capital, but banks are structured to provide loans for relatively short fixed periods. Companies draw these down but they rarely eliminate them. They simply replace them with new loans.

However, each time a company goes looking for new funds it must prove itself to be credit worthy; it must show strong evidence that it can service both the interest and principal.

In many ways, debt has features that are the opposite of equity: it is less costly, it does not dilute control, but it brings extra risk.

Sale of fixed assets

This can be a last resort. However, it may be the only way out of a liquidity crisis. Indeed, sometimes it can be a very beneficial move even in a non-crisis situation.

Matching of short-term and long-term liquidity

When we look at a company's liquidity position we must make a distinction between long-term and short-term sections of the balance sheet. Figure 7.6 shows the five-box balance sheet and highlights this distinction.

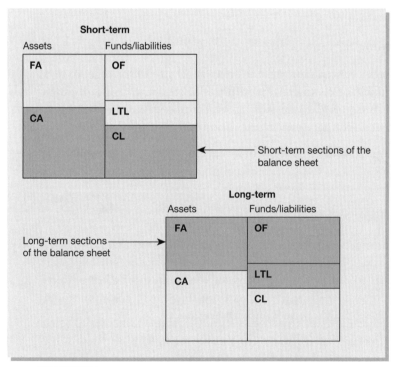

Figure 7.6   Long-term and short-term balance sheet analysis

'Current assets' and 'current liabilities' both fall into the short-term area. The remaining three boxes – 'owners' funds', 'long-term loans' and 'fixed assets' – occupy the long-term area.

A certain balance should exist between the long-term assets and funds on the one hand and the short-term assets and funds on the other. As a general rule, long-term assets in a company should be matched by corresponding long-term liabilities.

Alternative and contrasting positions

A balance sheet with its five boxes drawn to scale can highlight the profile of a company. By profile we mean the shape of the balance sheet in terms of the relative weight of each of the five boxes. These profiles are determined by the operating characteristics of the industrial sector in which a company operates.

Such profiles throw useful light on how a company will respond to certain conditions. Companies that are heavy in current assets will be adversely affected by an increase in the rate of inflation

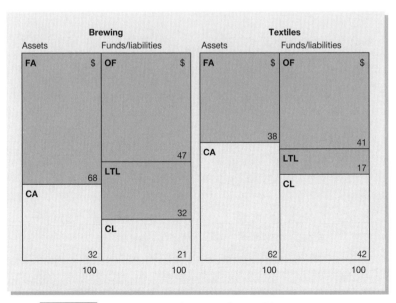

Figure 7.7 Alternative and contrasting positions

very quickly. Companies that have borrowed heavily are, of course, very responsive to changes in overall levels of interest rates.

Examples of two contrasting companies are shown in Figure 7.7. On the left we see the balance sheet outline of a company from the brewing sector. A very high percentage of the total assets are in the long-term investment area and there is a corresponding reliance on equity and long-term loans.

Short-term liquidity

This chapter reviews short-term liquidity measures:

- Current and quick ratio
- Working capital to sales
- Working capital days

Short-term liquidity measures

The first test of a company's financial position is, 'Will it have sufficient cash over the immediate future to meet its short-term liabilities as they fall due?' Unless the answer here is positive, the company is in a financial crisis irrespective of its profit performance.

Normally short-term liabilities amount to a considerable part of the total borrowings of the company. They are always greater than the company's physical cash resources. The question we ask is, 'Where will the cash come from to pay them?'

Cash is in constant movement through the company. It flows in frequently from accounts receivable as customers pay their bills. Each payment reduces the total accounts receivable balance outstanding, unless it is in turn topped up by transfers from the finished goods inventory as new sales are made. The finished goods inventory is likewise fed from raw materials and work in process. We can visualise these assets as temporary stores for cash, i.e. inventories in various forms and accounts receivable. These are the assets that collectively make up 'current assets'. They amount to a high percentage of a company's total investment.

At the same time, goods are being purchased on credit from suppliers, thereby creating short-term liabilities. Normally other short-term loans are being used as well. It is these that we collectively refer to as 'current liabilities'.

We measure a firm's short-term liquidity position by comparing the values of 'current assets' with its 'current liabilities'.

There are three key ways of evaluating this relationship:

- the current and quick ratios
- 'working capital to sales' ratio
- working capital days.

 ## Current ratio

The current ratio is a favourite of the institutions that lend money. The calculation is based on a simple comparison between the totals of 'current assets' and 'current liabilities'.

Current assets represent the amount of liquid, i.e. cash and near-cash, assets available to a business. Current liabilities give an indication of its upcoming cash requirements. Institutions expect to see a positive cash surplus. We therefore look for a value comfortably in excess of 1.0 for this ratio. While this is the standard for most types of businesses, certain types of operation are capable of operating at a much lower value.

In Figure 8.1 we can see that the current ratio for the Example Co. plc is 1.3 times.

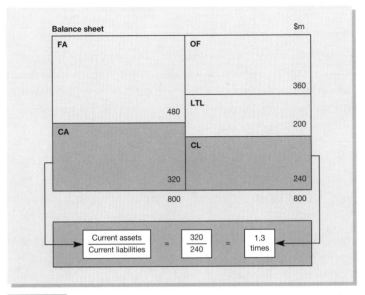

Figure 8.1 Current ratio applied to data from the Example Co. plc

A word of caution is needed concerning the interpretation of this or any other ratio for a particular company. A wide diversity of conditions exist in different types of business. Some businesses are able to exist comfortably with liquidity ratios that would spell disaster for others. Some companies have to carry large stocks, have long production cycles and offer long credit to customers. Other businesses carry almost no stock and receive more credit from suppliers than they give to customers.

One ratio value in isolation tells us little. To get a good picture of a situation we must use a series of tests and we must apply appropriate benchmarks. These benchmarks can be derived from many sources, such as historical data, competitors' accounts and published data of all kinds.

It can be said, regarding liquidity ratios, that it is the trend over time rather than the absolute value that gives the most valuable information. A current ratio of 1.3 could give either a good or bad signal depending on past results.

A disadvantage of this ratio is that it does not distinguish between different types of current assets, some of which are far more liquid than others. A company could be getting into cash problems and still have a strong current ratio. This issue is somewhat addressed by the next ratio.

 ## Quick ratio

The calculation here is very similar to that of the 'current ratio'. Simply remove the 'inventories' value from the 'current assets' and divide the result by the 'current liabilities' total.

The reason for excluding the inventory figure is that its liquidity can be a problem. You will recall that the term 'liquidity' is used to express how quickly, and to what percentage of its book value, an asset can be converted into cash if the need were to arise.

For instance, a cargo of crude oil in port at Rotterdam has a high liquidity value, whereas rolls of material for making fashion garments stored in a warehouse probably have a low liquidity value.

We can meet with a situation where a company has a constant current but a falling quick ratio. This would be a most dangerous sign. It tells us that inventory is building up at the expense of receivables and cash.

Lending institutions have difficulty in ascertaining the liquidity of many types of inventory. They feel much more comfortable when dealing with receivables and cash. Accordingly they pay quite a lot of attention to the 'quick ratio'.

Both the current and quick ratios are the most widely used measures of short-term liquidity but a problem with them is that they are static. They reflect values at a point in time only, i.e. at the balance sheet date. It is possible to 'window dress' a company's accounts so that it looks good on this one day only. To deal with this shortcoming it is argued that cash flow over the short-term future would be a better indicator of ability to pay. The 'working capital to sales' ratio covered next meets this objection to a certain extent.

In Figure 8.2 we can see that the quick ratio for the Example Co. plc is 0.8 times.

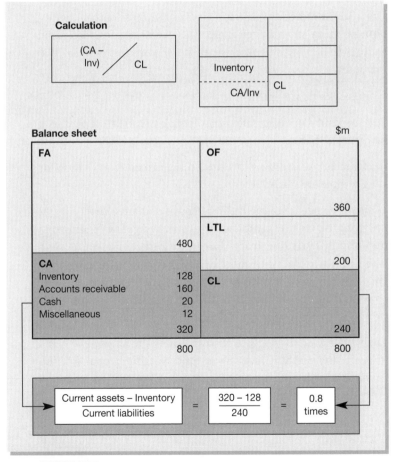

Figure 8.2   Quick ratio applied to data from the Example Co. plc

A value of 1.0 is usually very strong. It means that the company can pay off all its short-term liabilities from its cash balances plus its accounts receivable. Most companies decide that such a level of liquidity is unnecessary. An alternative name for this ratio is the 'acid test' ratio.

 ## Working capital to sales ratio

The working capital to sales ratio gives us a glimpse of the liquidity position from yet another angle. This measure shows up some features that cannot be ascertained easily from the previous two measures.

Working capital is 'current assets' less 'current liabilities'.

The working capital to sales ratio looks at working capital as a percentage of 'sales'.

In Figure 8.3 we can see that the working capital to sales ratio for the Example Co. plc is 7%.

Whereas the current and quick ratios use balance sheet figures only, here we take into account the ongoing operations by including a value from the profit and loss account. The 'sales' figure reflects, to some extent, the operating cash flow through the whole system. This ratio, therefore, relates the short-term surplus liquidity to the annual operating cash flow.

The working capital to sales ratio indicates the amount of cents in every dollar that is required to fund working capital. For the Example Co. plc, illustrated in Figure 8.2, this would be 7 cents in every dollar, which is very low.

Cash flows from managing working capital, essentially the cash received from customers after paying off its bills and short-term debts, is an essential source of short-term operational finance for a business. As sales grow, working capital or the cash required to

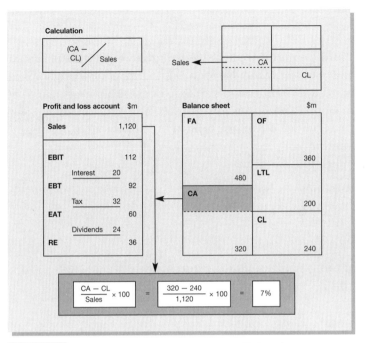

Figure 8.3 Working capital to sales ratio applied to data from the Example Co. plc

finance operational expenses should usually grow in the same proportion. Therefore changes in the working capital to sales ratio should be investigated further.

This will often highlight a trend the other ratios miss. It is possible to have a stable 'current' or 'quick' ratio while this ratio is falling. This would happen if sales were increasing rapidly but levels of working capital were static. A condition known as 'overtrading' could develop.

The term 'overtrading' is used to describe a situation where there are not sufficient liquid resources in the balance sheet to meet comfortably the day-to-day cash needs of the existing level of business. It arises in a company that has grown too fast or has been underfunded in the first place. The symptoms show up as a constant shortage of cash to meet day-to-day needs.

There is a danger of bankruptcy. Probably the only solution to the condition is an injection of long-term liquid funds.

There is a difference between being short of 'working capital' and managing the business so that less 'working capital' is needed. The latter is a sign of good management. The modern trend is towards a lower 'working capital to sales' ratio, particularly in the form of much reduced inventories. A low, but not too low, working capital to sales ratio can be an indication of efficiency.

Please note that some businesses use the reciprocal of this ratio, i.e. sales to working capital.

 ## Working capital days

Possibly the clearest way of looking at the role of working capital in a company's operations is through working capital days.

We saw this concept in passing in Chapter 6 when we looked at model variations for performance drivers.

We have used the term 'working capital' here to include three items only, i.e. 'inventory', 'accounts receivable' and 'accounts payable', whereas the classic definition of working capital covers all items in 'current assets' and 'current liabilities'. We only look at these three items because they are:

- the dominant accounts within working capital; and
- their behaviour is spontaneous – they react very quickly to changes in levels of company turnover.

The company will have policies regarding levels of inventory, accounts receivable and accounts payable. However, these policies will not fix the absolute values of these balances, which will be changed according to the level of sales. A sustained growth in sales, for example, will inevitably result in the growth of these three balances.

The main items excluded are 'cash' and 'short loans' which depend on policy decisions. For operating management purpose, this narrow definition is more useful.

We have used data from accounts of the Example Co. plc for 'inventory', 'accounts receivable' and 'accounts payable'. Each category is divided by sales and then multiplied by 365 days. This calculates the number of days of each category – for example, how many days the business holds inventory, how many days it takes to collect receipts from customers and how many days it takes to pay its suppliers.

The calculations are shown below:

Inventory days

$$\frac{\text{Inventories}}{\text{Sales}} \times 365 = \frac{128}{1,120} \times 365 = 42 \text{ days}$$

Accounts receivable days

$$\frac{\text{Accounts receivable}}{\text{Sales}} \times 365 = \frac{160}{1,120} \times 365 = 52 \text{ days}$$

Accounts payable days

$$\frac{\text{Accounts payable}}{\text{Sales}} \times 365 = \frac{140}{1,120} \times 365 = 46 \text{ days}$$

We have plotted this data in Figure 8.4, which is an interesting representation of the operating cash cycle time gap. The objective is to show the number of days that elapse from the time money is paid out to the suppliers of materials until the corresponding cash is received back from the customer that buys the goods.

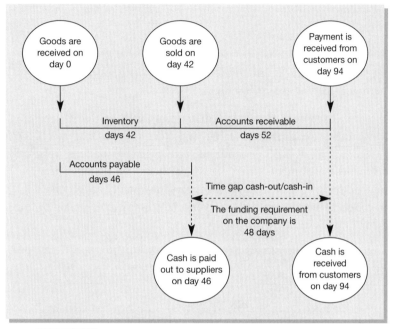

Figure 8.4 **Working capital days for the Example Co. plc**

We nominate day 0 to indicate when goods are received from suppliers. Given the average stockholding period, day 42 indicates when the goods are sold. The customer takes on average 52 days to pay, so cash is received on day 94.

In the meantime the company, given its average number of days credit, will have paid the supplier on day 46. The time gap between the cash out on day 46 and its return to the company on day 94 is 48 days. (In addition the company will have paid out in respect of wages, salaries and overheads all through the period.)

It is this time gap that creates in a company the need for working capital. The amount is easily quantified. Given a gap of 48 days, each $1m of sales requires 'about' $131,500 ($1m × 48/365) of working capital. Every increase of $1m will create a need for an additional $131,500 in cash resources. This point is often missed by small rapidly growing companies who find themselves in cash difficulties in the midst of high sales and profits. This is typical of 'overtrading' companies.

The working capital days ratios are often categorised as 'efficiency' ratios as they are useful indicators of how efficient management are in running a business.

Financial strength

This chapter reviews measures of financial strength:

- Interest cover
- Debt to equity ratio
- Leverage

By 'financial strength' we mean a company's ability to withstand operating setbacks. In the previous chapter we looked at the short-term position. The long-term situation is even more important.

 Interest cover

This ratio is derived solely from the profit and loss account. It measures a company's ability to service its borrowings.

The 'interest' charge is divided into the 'EBIT' figure to give the 'cover' expressed as 'so many times'.

Three factors determine the level of 'interest cover:

■ the operating profit
■ the total amount borrowed
■ the effective rate of interest.

A highly profitable company can have adequate interest cover even though the balance sheet may appear to show a high level of borrowing.

The level of interest rates in an economy will impinge significantly on this ratio, which may partly explain why low-interest economies seem to accept more highly leveraged balance sheets.

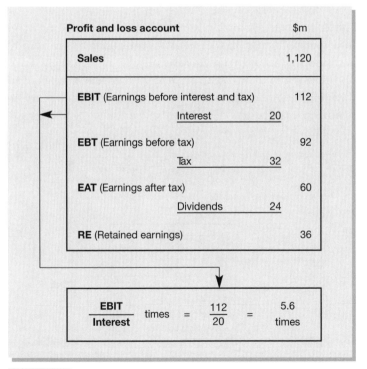

Figure 9.1   Interest cover applied to data from the Example
Co. plc

The term 'financial leverage' is used to reflect the relationship between profit and the fixed interest charge. A high financial leverage, where interest is a high part of pre-interest profits, is an indicator of risk. A small change in operating profit will have a greatly magnified effect on the return to shareholders. A highly leveraged company does well in boom times, but quickly falls into difficulty in a recession.

We can see in Figure 9.1 that the interest cover for the Example Co. plc is 5.6 times. A prudent value for a company is around 5 times.

'Debt to equity' ratio (D/E)

The 'debt to equity' ratio is one of the most fundamental measures in corporate finance. It is a great test of the financial strength of a company. Although used universally, it unfortunately turns up under many different names and with different methods of calculation. This causes some confusion which we will try to remove in this chapter.

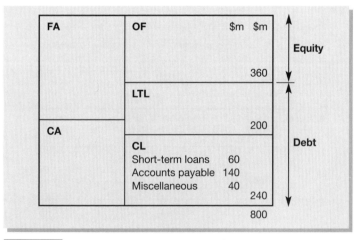

Figure 9.2   The debt to equity ratio

The purpose of the ratio is to measure the mix of funds in the balance sheet and to make a comparison between those funds that have been supplied by the owners (equity) and those which have been borrowed (debt). This distinction is illustrated in Figure 9.2.

The idea seems a very simple one. Nevertheless difficulties arise in two areas:

■ 'What do we mean by debt?'

■ 'How exactly will we express the calculation?'

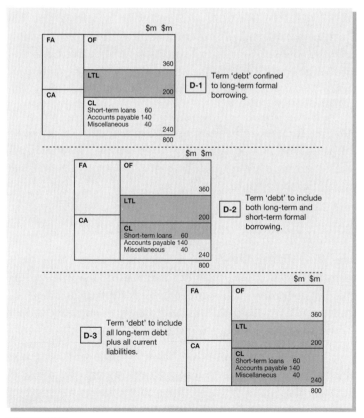

Figure 9.3   Different definitions of debt

We will first consider different meanings given to the term 'debt'. In Figure 9.3 you will see the three interpretations in common use:

- long-term loans only
- long-term and short-term loans (i.e. all interest-bearing debt)
- long-term loans plus all current liabilities (i.e. total debt).

Note that the first two definitions concentrate on formal interest-bearing debt, i.e. that sourced from banks or other financial institutions. In bank calculations, these are the definitions most commonly used. The final definition includes trade creditors plus all accruals, such as dividends, tax and other miscellaneous amounts.

The reason bank analysts use the more restricted view of debt is understandable. Their claims usually rank ahead of trade and other creditors. From the banks' point of view, the only debt that matters is that which ranks equal to or ahead of their own position.

However, from the companies' viewpoint, debt due to a supplier is just as real and as important as that due to a bank. There are therefore good arguments for including all debt in the calculation of the debt to equity ratio.

How to calculate the debt to equity ratio

As stated, one kind of debt is as important as another from a management point of view. For that reason, we will use the broadest definition – long-term loans plus current liabilities – for the remainder of this book. This done, we will examine the various ways in which the ratio can be calculated.

First we should emphasise that it matters little which method of calculation we use. Different methods simply give different numbers that mean the same thing. We can measure length in either inches or centimetres and the different numbers express the same length. Similarly, we can express the relationship between equity and debt in different ways. The true ratio is the same irrespective of how it is expressed.

This point is worth noting. Despite an appearance of dozens of business ratios of all kinds, there are actually a relatively small number of independent financial ratios that are absolutely fundamental. The 'debt to equity' ratio is once such ratio.

Figure 9.4 illustrates three methods for expressing the 'debt to equity' ratio:

Method 1 – debt over equity

This is the classic approach and it is used widely, i.e. all formal interest-bearing debt is expressed as a ratio to equity. However, from the answer it gives it is often difficult to visualise the total balance sheet.

When a debt to equity value is quoted for a company, then, in the absence of evidence to the contrary, it should be assumed that this method has been adopted.

As opposed to a percentage this is often expressed as a traditional ratio. For Example Co. plc 'debt *over* equity' of 72% could also be expressed as 'debt *to* equity' of 0.72 times.

Method 2 – equity over total funds

An approach that is not so common. The answer is almost the reciprocal of the third method shown below, which is more often encountered.

Method 3 – total debt over total funds

This approach can be the easiest to understand, i.e. all debt in the balance sheet (whether interest-bearing or not) is expressed as a percentage of total funds. The answer shows directly the percentage of the balance sheet funded by debt. It therefore gives an instant picture of the funding side of the total balance sheet.

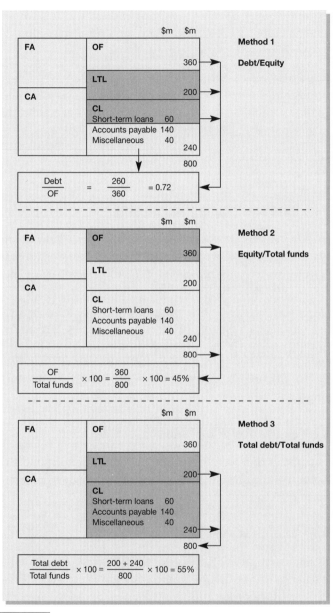

Figure 9.4 Different methods of expressing the debt to equity ratio

A hybrid approach

We will return to the debt to equity ratio in Chapter 12 (the corporate valuation model) where we will use a hybrid of the above methods.

The numbers are easily extracted from the most complex set of accounts.

The importance of the debt to equity ratio

We place a lot of emphasis on this ratio because, if it goes wrong, the company has a real long-term problem; one which may become terminal.

The greater the debt, the greater the risk. All debt in the balance sheet gives third parties legal claims on the company. These claims are for interest payments at regular intervals, plus repayment of the principal by the agreed time. The principal is repaid either by periodic instalments or a single lump sum at the end of the loan period.

Therefore when a company raises debt, it takes on a commitment to substantial fixed cash outflows for some time into the future. The company does not have a guaranteed cash inflow over the same period. Indeed the inflow may be most uncertain. A fixed cash outflow combined with an uncertain cash inflow gives rise to financial risk. It follows that the greater the loan, the greater is the risk.

Why, then, do companies take on debt and incur this extra risk? The answer lies in the relative costs. Debt costs less than equity funds. By adding debt to its balance sheet, a company can generally improve its profitability, add to its share price, increase the wealth of its shareholders and develop greater potential for growth.

Debt increases both profit and risk. It is the job of management to maintain a proper balance between the two.

Where should the line be drawn? The increased risk to the equity shareholder that results from debt leverage can rarely be forgotten altogether even though some companies do just that. Most companies must take a view on the degree of uncertainty of future cash receipts and arrange their level of debt in line with this uncertainty.

Companies in business sectors with very predictable income streams, e.g. property leasing, usually incur high levels of debt. Companies in highly volatile sectors, e.g. mine exploration, usually fund mainly from equity.

Variations in the levels of debt will also occur across countries and according to the state of the economy. Much has been written exploring the reasons for these variations. The general conclusion seems to be that they arise because of attitudinal, cultural and historical, rather than financial, factors.

Leverage

It is interesting to consider the impact of different debt to equity ratios on shareholders' returns.

In Figure 9.5, we see a company for which the mix of funds has not yet been decided. (Note: This is a different example to the illustrative 'Example Co. plc' we are using elsewhere in this book.) It has assets of $100,000, sales of $120,000 and an operating profit of $15,000. The effects of different levels of gearing or leverage on the shareholders are illustrated in Figures 9.6 and 9.7. (Note: For simplicity, tax is ignored and the interest rate is set at 10%.)

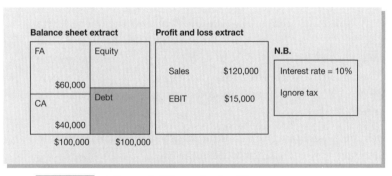

Figure 9.5   Effects of different levels of leverage

In Figure 9.6 just one level of leverage is analysed to illustrate how the figures work. Option 1 in the first row illustrates a situation with $100,000 equity and no debt. Accordingly there is no interest charge. The total profit of $15,000 is applied to the shareholders' investment of $100,000. The ROE is 15%.

In the second row, the funding mix has changed to $80,000 equity and $20,000 debt. The interest charge at 10% is $2,000. This is deducted from the profit of $15,000 to leave $13,000 for the shareholders. Because the equity investment is now $80,000 the ROE is 16.25% ($13,00/$80,000 × 100).

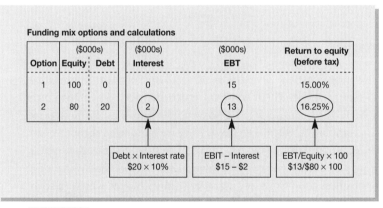

Figure 9.6　Funding mix options and calculations

As a result of introducing 20% debt into the company, the ROE has increased from 15% to 16.25%. This is financial leverage in action.

In Figure 9.7, the leverage has been extended in steps all the way up to 90%. With each additional slice of debt, the ROE increases until it reaches 60% at the 90% level of debt. Extraordinarily high levels of return can thus be achieved from very highly leveraged companies. The price that is paid for these high returns is the additional exposure to risk.

Degrees of leverage and impact on ROE

Option	($000s) Equity	Debt	Interest	EBT	Return to equity (before tax)
1	100	0	0	15	15.00%
2	80	20	2	13	16.25%
3	60	40	4	11	18.33%
4	50	50	5	10	20.00%
5	40	60	6	9	22.50%
6	20	80	8	7	35.00%
7	10	90	9	6	**60.00%**

Figure 9.7 Degrees of leverage and impact on ROE

Summary

The debt/equity or leverage decision is one of great importance to management. There is a risk–return trade-off. The impulse to achieve high returns for the shareholders must be restrained by the company's risk profile. Even a very well managed company can suffer an unexpected deterioration in its financial position either from a default on the part of a major debtor or a general worsening of business conditions. It can be very difficult to recover from such a deterioration. It is prudent to balance leverage and to keep some liquidity in reserve to guard against such an eventuality.

10

The cash flow statement

This chapter reviews:

- Cash versus profit
- The cash flow statement

For purposes of completeness we have included a chapter on the cash flow statement. This statement is used more externally than internally to analyse a business.

The cash flow statement completes a company's set of published accounts. Its purpose is to track the flow of funds through the company. It identifies where cash has gone to and where it has come from and it is a very powerful tool for explaining movements in the various liquidity ratios.

Cash versus profit

The rules relating to cash flow are very simple. Every time a company pays out cash, writes a cheque or makes a bank transfer, a cash outflow occurs. When cash, a cheque or a bank transfer is received, there is a cash inflow. This is the only rule, and its very simplicity means that it is difficult to find mechanisms to hide unpleasant truths about a company's affairs.

Many operating cash movements do not appear in the profit and loss account. One reason is that the profit and loss account uses the accruals concept to adjust a company's cash flows to bring them into line with revenue earned and costs incurred for a specific period. While it is most important that true revenue and costs are identified, these adjustments sometimes hide important aspects of a company's affairs.

There are those who would contend that the cash flow statement is more reliable and less subject to manipulation than the profit and loss account.

However, despite its clarity, it cannot, as is occasionally suggested, replace the profit and loss account. The profit and loss account correctly distinguishes between cash paid for electricity consumed in the last month and cash paid for a building that will be occupied by the company for the next 20 years.

The format of the cash flow statement

The cash flow statement has historically been presented in many formats and is now relatively standardised across accounting jurisdictions.

The purpose of the cash flow statement is to reconcile opening and closing cash balances.

The statement presents this reconciliation under the following headings:

- operating activities
- servicing of finance and taxation
- investing activities
- financing activities.

Figure 10.1 identifies the main headings in a cash flow statement but omits much of the detail in the interest of clarity.

Operating activities

An important number in the cash flow statement is the 'net cash inflow (or outflow) from operating activities' within the first section on operating activities.

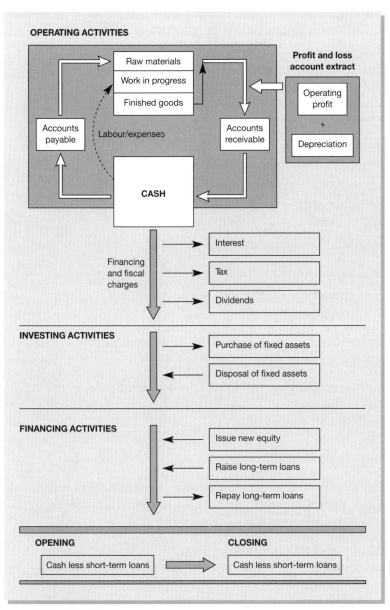

Figure 10.1   Main headings of a corporate cash flow report

It is interesting to compare this to a business's operating profit (or EBIT). A healthy operating profit does not always equate to a healthy cash flow from operating activities. In the long run, for a stable business, there should be a correlation between cash and profit; however, in the short term there can be differences. These differences are highlighted here.

There will be a supporting note to this section of the cash flow statement which reconciles the operating profit to the cash flow from operations. This will account for movements in working capital as well as any non-cash items such as depreciation.

Servicing of finance and taxation

This section of the cash flow statement shows:

- interest paid
- tax paid
- dividends paid.

It shows the outflows required to satisfy the funders of the business as well as the tax authorities.

For some businesses there may also be interest receipts and dividend receipts from various investments shown under this heading.

Investing activities

This section of the cash flow statement shows the purchase and sale of assets. This can include fixed assets, such as new buildings, as well as investments in other businesses.

It is useful to see if a business is investing in its future. Business growth should be supported by investment in new long-term assets.

Financing activities

This section of the cash flow statement focuses on any changes in business funding. New equity issues or the refinancing of debt will be shown here.

Essentially the financial statements should tell a story of what is happening to a business. Any changes in financing should be supported by changes elsewhere in the business.

For example, a business may have raised a new loan to pay for a new factory to meet growing demand. This is positive news and should result in higher profits in future years.

The terminology from the cash flow statement is widely used in boardrooms and management meetings. It is important that managers be familiar with this terminology and appreciate the significance of the various components of cash flow.

four

Corporate value

Investor ratios

This chapter reviews:

- Share values, earnings per share and the price to earnings ratio
- Dividends per share, dividend cover and the pay-out ratio
- Earnings and dividend yields
- Market to book ratio

Introduction

The value of public companies is determined by the stock market. The value of companies not publicly quoted will be greatly influenced by the same market. In this chapter, therefore, we will look at the main stock-market-related ratios.

These are:

- share values (nominal, book and market)
- earnings per share (EPS)
- dividends per share (DPS)
- dividend cover and the pay-out ratio
- earnings yield

- dividend yield
- price to earnings ratio (P/E)
- market to book ratio.

When people talk about the value of a company they mean its market capitalisation or the combined value of the common stock. We have already looked at the position that common shares occupy in the balance sheet and have seen where they stand in the queue for participation in profits. Both these issues are important for an understanding of this chapter.

Figure 11.1 shows the balance sheet for the Example Co. plc. The top right-hand box shows owners' funds totalling $360m. Various accounting rules have been applied over many years in arriving at this value, e.g. how much depreciation has been charged to the profit and loss account?

Balance sheet				$m	
Long-term investment	$	$	**Owners' funds**	$	$
Intangibles	0		Issued capital	80	
Net fixed assets	440		Capital reserves	60	
Investments	40		Revenue reserves	220	
					360
			Long-term loans		
		480			
					200
Current assets					
Inventory	128		**Current liabilities**		
Accounts receivable	160		Short-term loans	60	
Cash	20		Accounts payable	140	
Miscellaneous	12		Miscellaneous	40	
		320			240
		800			800

Figure 11.1 Company valuation applied to data from the Example Co. plc

A more pragmatic approach to determine the value of owners' funds is to take the total assets figure of $800m and deduct from it the total liabilities figure of $440m (200 + 240). This approach gives us the same answer in our example but it emphasises the importance of the asset values in determining shareholders' funds. The authentic value for owners' funds is derived simply by taking the total value of all assets in today's terms and deducting all third party liabilities.

While all asset values can be queried, and one or two liabilities, the main areas where difficulties can be expected are:

- fixed assets
- inventories
- certain liabilities.

Fixed assets

How realistic are the values? We are primarily interested in value-in-use, but there are occasions when break-up value is important.

Inventories

These very often present difficulty in determining the appropriate value. When we place a value on inventory we are making a judgement about future trading conditions. We are assuming that the value shown will be realised.

Certain liabilities

There may be liabilities or potential liabilities which have not been provided for, e.g. pension liabilities that are not fully funded.

Share values

In Chapter 2, three types of share value were mentioned in passing. We now look at these in detail using figures from the Example Co. plc (Figure 11.2).

There are 32 million issued common shares, for each of which there is a:

- nominal (par) value of $2.50
- book (asset) value of $11.25
- market value of $22.50.

Let us now look at each of these in turn.

Nominal (par or face) value

The nominal value is largely a notional low figure arbitrarily placed on a company's stock. It serves to determine the value of 'issued common stock', i.e. in the Example Co. plc the number of issued shares is 32 million. The par value is $2.50 to give a value of $80m. If new shares are issued, they will hold this same nominal value even though the issue price will probably be much above it, close to the current market price. If new shares are issued at a price of, say, $17.50, there is a surplus of $15.00 over the nominal value. This surplus is called the 'share premium' and it forms part of the capital reserves. Many companies today have shares of 'no par value' for simplicity. They simply put it in the books at their original sale price.

Book value (asset value, or asset backing)

This value is arrived at by dividing the number of issued shares – 32 million – into the owners' funds of $360m. The book value of all the shares is $360m. Therefore each share has a book value

Share data

No of $2.50 common shares = 32,000,000

Market price of share = $22.50

Example Co. plc

Balance sheet					$m
Long-term investment	$	$	**Owners' funds**	$	$
Intangibles	0		Issued capital	80	
Net fixed assets	440		Capital reserves	60	
Investments	40		Revenue reserves	220	
					360
			Long-term loans		
		480			
					200
Current assets			**Current liabilities**		
Inventory	128		Short-term loans	60	
Accounts receivable	160		Accounts payable	140	
Cash	20		Miscellaneous	40	
Miscellaneous	12	320			240
		800			800

Book value per share

Total owners' funds = $360,000,000
Number of common shares = 32,000,000

Book value per share = $11.25 ($360/32)
(Also known as the share *asset backing*.)

Market capitalisation

Number of common shares = 32,000,000
Market value per share = $22.50

Market capitalisation = $720,000,000

Figure 11.2 Share value and market capitalisation applied to data from the Example Co. plc of \$11.25. We discussed earlier the need to validate the value of \$360m. For instance, if an examination of the inventories produced a more prudent valuation of \$20m less than the balance sheet value (\$108m), this write-down would reduce the owners' funds from \$360m to \$340m. The book value would fall from \$11.25 to \$10.625 per share.

Market value \$22.50

This is the price quoted on a stock market for a public company or an estimated price for a non-quoted company. The stock market price will constantly change in response to actual or anticipated results. Media commentary and overall market sentiment will also impact on the share price. The main objective of company management is usually to maintain the best share price possible under any set of conditions.

Market value can be expressed per share (usually referred to as share price) or for the company as a whole (usually referred to as market capitalisation).

These different values will be used to derive the various ratios explored in the rest of the chapter.

Earnings per share (EPS)

'Earnings per share' is one of the most widely quoted statistics when there is a discussion of a company's performance or share value.

Figure 11.3 shows how this ratio is calculated. Remember that the common shareholder comes last in the queue for participating in profit. The profit used in the calculation is the figure after all other claimants have been satisfied. The most common prior charges in the profit and loss account are interest and tax.

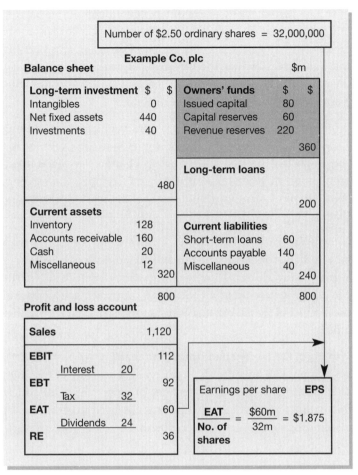

Figure 11.3 Earnings per share for the Example Co. plc

Therefore it is the earnings after tax (EAT) figure that is divided by the number of common shares to calculate the value of earnings per share. This figure tells us what profit has been earned by the common shareholder for every share held.

It serves no purpose to compare the earnings per share in one company with that in another because a company can elect to have a large number of shares of low denomination or a smaller number of a higher denomination. A company can also decide to increase or reduce the number of shares on issue. This decision will automatically alter the earnings per share. We cannot say, therefore, that a company with an earnings per share value of 50¢ is any better than one with a value of 40¢.

While the absolute amount of earnings per share tells nothing about a company's performance, the growth in EPS over time is a very important statistic. Indeed, many chairpersons stress it as a prime target in annual reports. Furthermore, growth in earnings per share has a significant influence on the market price of the share.

Growth in EPS tells us more about a company's progress than growth in absolute profits. Growth in profits can result from a great many things. However, following a share issue, if the percentage increase in profit is less than the percentage increase in the number of shares, earnings per share will fall even with higher profits.

Stability of EPS is often more important than growth and potential volatility in EPS. Investors look closely at the quality of earnings. They dislike the erratic performance of companies with widely fluctuating profits. A high-quality rating is given to earnings that are showing steady, non-volatile growth.

 ## Dividends per share (DPS)

Figure 11.4 shows how to calculate this value. Only a proportion of the earnings accruing to the shareholders is paid out to them in cash. The remainder is retained to consolidate and expand the business.

It is a well-established rule that dividends are paid only out of profits, not from any other source. However, the earnings need not necessarily fall into the same year as the dividends. Therefore

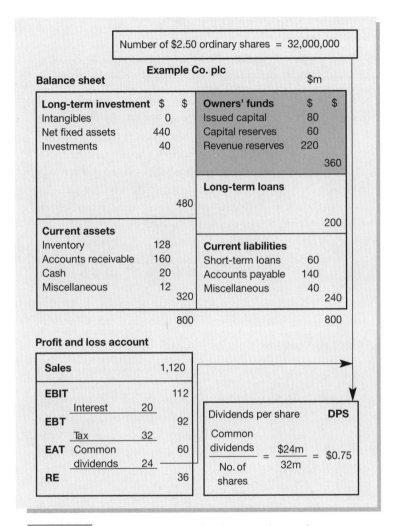

Figure 11.4   Dividends per share for the Example Co. plc

situations can arise when dividends exceed earnings. In such cases, dividends are being paid from earnings that have been retained in the business from previous years.

The total return to the shareholder over any given time consists of the dividend received plus the growth in the share price. While for some investors growth is most important, many shareholders and potential investors – both private individuals and institutions such as pension funds which need income for their day-to-day affairs – pay very close attention to dividends. They look at the absolute dividend per share and for a history of stable but growing payments.

Therefore companies dislike intensely having to reduce the dividend because this will drive away investors with possibly serious effects on share price. A company in a difficult year will often decide that it must pay a dividend in excess of earnings rather than cut the pay-out. Of course, this policy can be followed only for a short time and when there is reason to believe that earnings will recover to a figure greater than the dividends. It should also be noted that it is illegal for a company to pay a dividend unless there are sufficient distributable reserves.

Dividend cover and the pay-out ratio

These two ratios are mirror images of one another and give the same information. Both express the relationship between a company's earnings and the cash paid out in dividends. Figure 11.5 shows the calculations. For the first ratio divide EPS by DPS. For the second reverse the numbers.

Companies adopt dividend policies to suit their business needs. These will reflect the sectors in which they operate and the specific strategies they adopt. Fast-growing companies have a great need for cash and they pay out little. On the other hand stable low-growth companies usually pay out a higher percentage of earnings.

Public utility companies, for example, usually follow high stable pay-out policies. These companies attract investors for whom income is the most important consideration. As a contrasting example, some technology-based companies have never paid a dividend,

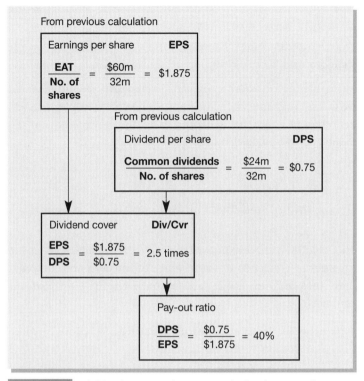

Figure 11.5 Dividend cover and pay-out ratio for the Example Co. plc

even though they have made large profits over many years. These companies attract investors who look for capital growth.

The importance of the dividend cover is the indication it gives of the future stability and growth of the dividend:

▪ A high cover (low pay-out ratio) suggests that the dividend is fairly safe, because it can be maintained in the face of any expected downturn in profit.

▪ A high cover also indicates a high retention policy, which suggests that the company is aiming for high growth.

It is worthwhile considering the implication of the pay-out ratio. The pay-out ratio shown in Figure 11.5 of 40% tells us that 60% of available profit is retained and hopefully invested back into the business. If companies retain more profits than they distribute, more than 50% of equity returns should come from capital growth, not dividends. However, capital growth depends on the share price.

Most share prices show significant fluctuations around a central trend line. Therefore, the actual capital gain delivered to a particular investor is heavily dependent on the timing of the investment and its later conversion back into cash.

Earnings and dividend yield ratios

The yield on a share expresses the return it provides in terms of earnings or dividends as a percentage of the current share price. Both measures are important for both the investor and the company.

Figure 11.6 shows calculations for the Example Co. plc.

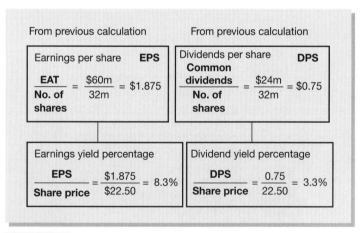

Figure 11.6   Share yield ratios for the Example Co. plc

The earnings yield shows the relationship that EPS bears to the share price. For instance, if the EPS is $1.50 and the share price is $10.00 the earnings yield is 15%. If the share price moved up to

$15.00 the corresponding yield would be 10%. As the share price increases the yield falls. Paradoxically, a low yield indicates a share that is in much demand by investors. We will see in the next section its link to the price to earnings ratio.

From the company's point of view, the ratio indicates the return the company must provide to attract investors. If a company falls out of favour in the market-place the share price falls and the company is faced with a higher yield. It follows that a company with a poor image has to pay a high return to attract capital.

For the investor, yield calculations allow comparisons to be made between the return on shares and other types of investment, such as government stocks (gilts) or commercial property.

Managers of large investment funds constantly balance their portfolios between these different investment outlets. In doing so, they take account of the relative yields which change daily, together with the stability and capital growth expected in each area.

Whereas the earnings yield specifies the total return, the dividend yield is more important for investors dependent on income from the shares. It allows them to compare the cash flow that they will receive from investing a fixed sum in different stocks or other investment outlets. As mentioned earlier, public utility companies tend to have high dividend pay-out ratios and therefore have high dividend yields which are popular with certain pension fund managers.

 ## Price to earnings ratio (P/E)

The price to earnings ratio or 'multiple' is a widely quoted parameter of share value. Figure 11.7 shows the method of calculation. The share price is divided by the EPS figure. The answer is the multiple of last year's earnings that the market is prepared to pay for a share today.

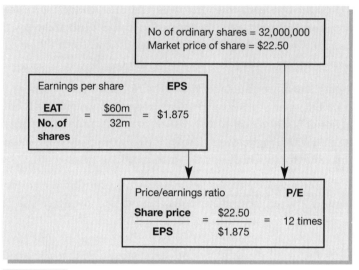

Figure 11.7 Price/earnings ratios for the Example Co. plc

While the calculation of the ratio is based on figures from the past, its value is determined by investors whose focus is on the future. They are primarily interested in the prospects for *earnings growth*. To estimate this they will look to the industrial sector, the company's products, its management and its financial stability and growth history.

The company has no direct control over the P/E ratio. It may influence it in the short term through good public relations. In the long term, however, it must deliver a good return to equity shareholders to secure a continued high rating.

The advantages of a high price to earnings ratio value are considerable:

■ The wealth of the company's owners is increased in proportion.

■ New funds can be raised at a favourable price.

■ The possibility of a successful hostile takeover bid is much reduced.

■ Most importantly, the company has the means to make acquisitions on favourable terms by using its 'paper' (shares), as opposed to cash.

The long-term historical average P/E ratio for all companies across all sectors is around 15. However, as this is an average there are naturally extremes with some high-growth technology-based companies achieving P/E ratios over 100. This is largely based on wild expectations of future growth. At the same time, these are often new businesses, and their earnings are relatively low, which helps to achieve such a high ratio.

 ## Market to book ratio

The market to book ratio gives the final, and perhaps the most thorough, assessment by the stock market of a company's overall status. It summarises the investors' view of the company overall, its management, its profits, its liquidity, and future prospects.

Figure 11.8 shows the calculation. The ratio relates the total market capitalisation of the company to the shareholders' funds. To express it in another way, it compares the value in the stock market with the shareholders' investment in the company.

The answer will be less than, greater than or equal to unity. It is the investors' perception of the performance of the company in terms of profits, balance sheet strength or liquidity and growth that determines this ratio.

A value of less than unity means that the shareholders' investment has diminished in value; it has wasted away. The investing community have given a 'thumbs down' signal to the company. They do not anticipate that future profits will be sufficient to justify the current owners' investment in the company.

On the other hand, when this value is well in excess of unity, it means that the investment has been multiplied by the market/book factor. A high ratio does not simply mean that the worth of the company has increased over time by means of its retained earnings. The multiplier acts in addition to this. Each $1 of original investment, plus each $1 of retained earnings is multiplied by a factor equal to the market to book ratio.

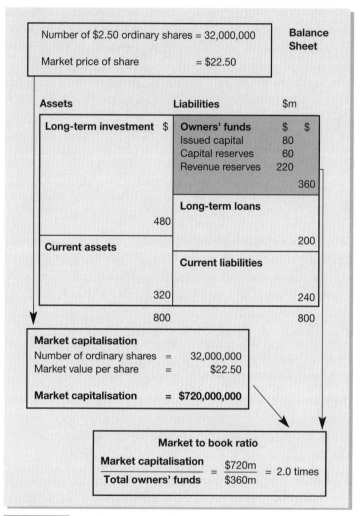

Figure 11.8 Market to book ratio for the Example Co. plc

Two important questions must be kept in mind when considering this ratio:

■ Do the shareholders' funds reflect a realistic value for the assets?

■ Is the market rating going through an exceptionally high or low phase?

In normal circumstances we would expect a value of between 2 and 3 times for this ratio. The US and the UK have historically experienced 'bull' markets with much higher multiples. This can be accounted for by:

- extraordinary exuberance in the market at certain times;
- the understatement of owners' equity as a result of goodwill write-downs.

Recessions or 'bear' markets will reduce these multiples considerably.

The absolute minimum that management must achieve for this ratio is 1.0. Good companies should produce a factor of 2.0 or more.

12

The corporate valuation model

This chapter reviews:

■ Financial leverage

■ Internal return versus required return

■ The importance of ROE

■ The corporate valuation model

Introduction

This chapter is a natural conclusion to all the previous chapters. It integrates the material and illustrates the relationships between many of the ratios. It does this through a single model of corporate value.

Specifically we will:

■ establish the financial leverage links between ROTA and ROE

■ examine further the great importance of ROE

■ tie together:

— operating efficiency measures

— leverage ratios

— valuation factors.

The overall aim of this chapter is to identify and quantify the drivers of corporate value.

To accomplish this we will make much use of the V chart (valuation chart).

Financial leverage

The popular term 'financial engineering' refers to schemes that aim to increase shareholders' return from a given return earned by a company.

The material that follows will give some appreciation of financial engineering.

The concept of leverage, or gearing, was covered briefly in Chapter 9 on financial strength. We demonstrated that high leverage could substantially increase the return to shareholders. This chapter will explore further the impact of leverage and the specific elements that link ROTA and ROE.

In Chapter 5 we calculated the following values for the Example Co. plc:

▨ ROTA 14.0%

▨ ROE 16.7%

Financial engineering has been used to transform a pre-tax (EBIT) return of 14.0% (ROTA) on the company's total assets into a post-tax (EAT) return of 16.7% (ROE) to shareholders. This is leverage in action.

Three financial variables link ROTA and ROE:

▨ debt to equity ratio

▨ average interest cost

▨ tax rate.

An explanation of each variable follows:

1. Debt to equity ratio

We looked at three methods of calculating the debt to equity ratio in Chapter 9 on financial strength. To demonstrate financial leverage we will use a hybrid approach which takes all debt (or non-equity funds) in the balance sheet (whether interest-bearing or not) and compares it to equity (owners' funds) expressed as a traditional ratio.

For Example Co. plc:

- Total debt (LTL + CL) = $440m
- Equity (OF) = $360m
- So the debt to equity ratio used here is: 1.2 times (440: 360).

2. Average interest cost

For this calculation we take the interest charge from the profit and loss account and divide it by total debt to give an 'average' interest charge on non-equity funds.

As this includes a number of 'free' funds in the balance sheet, e.g. accounts payable, the actual interest cost will inevitably be higher. However, the 'average' cost is specific to our demonstration.

For Example Co. plc:

- Interest = $20m
- Total debt (LTL + CL) = $440m
- So the average interest cost used here is 4.5%.

3. Tax rate

For this calculation we take the tax charge from the profit and loss account and divide it by pre-tax profit (EBT) to give an average tax rate for the year under consideration.

For Example Co. plc:

- Tax = $32m
- EBT = $92m
- So the average tax rate used here is 35%.

These three variables are laid out diagrammatically in Figure 12.1.

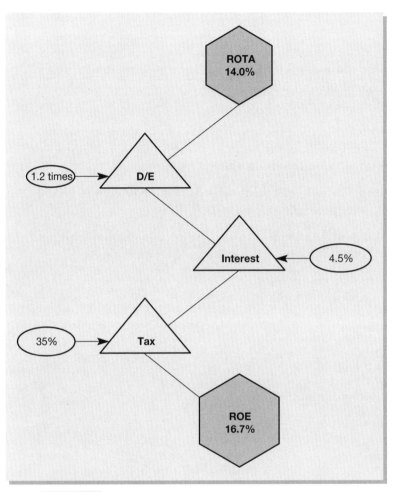

Figure 12.1 The links between return on total assets and return on equity

V chart

In Figure 12.2, a V chart (valuation chart) displays in geometric form the relationships between different performance measures for the Example Co. plc.

The V chart integrates in one diagram the financial variables that determine a company's valuation in the stock market.

The V chart looks formidable at first sight because there appear to be so many parts to it. However, we will work carefully through it. There are approximately six separate steps. Each step is simple in itself. The result of the exercise will be comprehension of quite a difficult subject. Once this is achieved the remaining material will be very easy to follow.

Step 1 The chart is constructed on a base that represents the total funds in the business divided between total equity ($360m) and total non-equity ($440m).

Step 2 Where equity and non-equity meet we draw to scale a vertical line representing ROTA (14%).

Step 3 At the extreme left of the base we place a vertical line representing the average cost of all non-equity funds – 4.5%.

Step 4 At the extreme right of the base we erect a vertical line to represent ROE (pre-tax) – 25.6%.

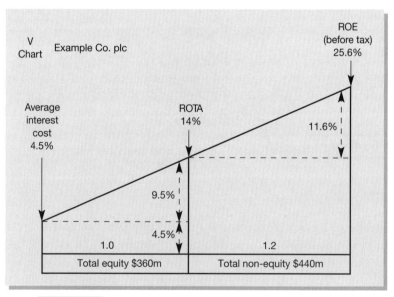

Figure 12.2   V chart for the Example Co. plc

Step 5 We join the upper limit of the 'Interest' line (Step 3) to the upper limit of the 'ROTA' line in the middle of the diagram (Step 2) and extend this diagonal to meet the ROE line on the right of the diagram (Step 4).

Step 6 The point where the diagonal line meets the right-hand vertical line represents ROE value (pre-tax).

ROE (pre-tax and post-tax)

ROE is normally calculated post-tax based on EAT. This is because the tax authorities must be paid before the shareholder.

In a V chart, however, we use ROE (pre-tax). This is simply to demonstrate the link between ROTA and ROE and the effects of the following three variables:

▪ debt to equity ratio

▪ average interest cost

▪ tax rate.

For Example Co. plc the calculations are as follows:

ROE (post-tax):

$$\frac{EAT}{OF} = \frac{60}{360} = 16.7\%$$

ROE (pre-tax):

$$\frac{EBT}{OF} = \frac{92}{360} = 25.6\%$$

We can move between ROE (pre-tax) and ROE (post-tax) with simple multiplication as follows:

ROE (post-tax) = ROE (pre-tax) × (1-tax rate)

16.7% = 25.6% × (1-35%)

(In the above calculation of ROE there is a small rounding difference with the figure of 16.7% as the tax rate is an average.)

V chart dynamics

To understand the dynamics of financial leverage, it is useful to imagine the V chart's diagonal line as a cantilevered beam which is anchored on the left vertical line.

The aim of the diagram is to demonstrate changes which impact on the ROE (pre-tax). The ROE (pre-tax) is represented by the height of the right-hand side of the V chart. This height is affected by the angle of the diagonal line.

The angle of the diagonal line and hence the size of the ROE (pre-tax) is determined by three factors:

1 The height of the left vertical line, or 'anchor', i.e. the average interest cost

2 The height of the centre vertical line, i.e. the ROTA value

3 The position of the centre vertical line, i.e. the relative values for 'equity' and 'non-equity'.

We can write this in an equation:

ROE (pre-tax) = ROTA + [(ROTA − Interest) × D/E]

25.6%   = 14.0% + [(14.0% − 4.5%)   × 1.2]

(In the above calculation of ROE there is a small difference due to rounding.) We can use either the chart or the formula to track a change in any of the input values to its effect on ROE (pre-tax).

Three examples are shown in Figure 12.3.

Example A: Increase ROTA by 1%

ROE (pre-tax) = ROTA + [(ROTA − Interest) × D/E]

27.6%   = 14.0% + [(15.0% − 4.5%)   × 1.2]

Example A demonstrates that a 1% increase in ROTA has a 2% positive impact on ROE (pre-tax).

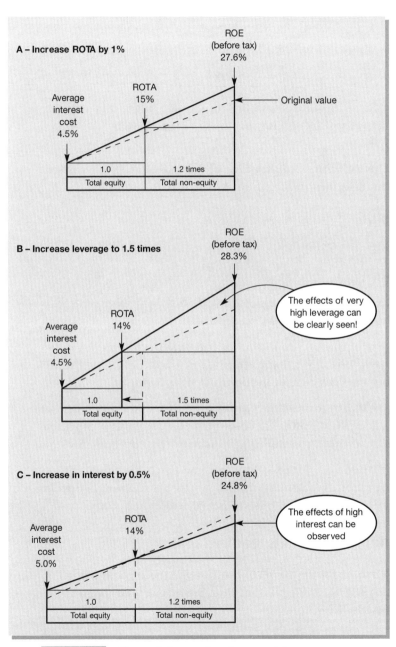

Figure 12.3 Effects of changes in values on V chart

Example B: Increase non-equity/equity to 1.5 times

ROE (pre-tax) = ROTA + [(ROTA − Interest) × D/E]

28.3%   = 14.0% + [(14.0% − 4.5%) × 1.5]

Example B demonstrates that an increase in the debt to equity ratio from 1.2 to 1.5 has an almost a 3% positive impact on ROE (pre-tax).

This shows that using leverage, or financial engineering, can substantially increase the return to shareholders.

Example C: Increase interest cost by 0.5%

ROE (pre-tax) = ROTA + [(ROTA − Interest) × D/E]

24.8%   = 14.0% + [(14.0% − 5.0%) × 1.2]

Example C demonstrates that a 0.5% increase in interest costs has an almost a 1% negative impact on ROE (pre-tax).

One of the risks of leverage is exposure to changes in interest rates. This shows that leverage is not without its risks. There is both upside potential and downside risk to consider.

The V chart approach has identified and quantified the variables that link the ROTA to ROE. The ones with the biggest impact and therefore the most important are ROTA and leverage (the debt/equity ratio).

Out next step is to link ROE to company value. When this is complete we will be able to trace a path from shop-floor variables right through to stock-market value. This is addressed in the next section.

Internal return versus required return

We looked at the market to book ratio in the previous chapter on investor ratios. We calculated this ratio using total company values as follows:

Market to book: $\dfrac{\text{Market capitalisation}}{\text{Owners' funds}} = \dfrac{\$720\text{m}}{\$360\text{m}} = 2 \text{ times}$

With the market/book ratio we express the relationship that exists between a company's value on the stock market and the underlying asset/book value as shown in the balance sheet. This ratio can be calculated for the company in total or for one share in the company.

As an alternative we can also perform the same calculation on a single-share basis.

First we need to calculate the book value per share:

$$\text{Book value per share: } \frac{\text{Owners' funds}}{\text{Number of shares}} = \frac{\$360\text{m}}{32\text{m}} = \$11.25$$

We then divide the share price by the book value per share:

$$\text{Market to book: } \frac{\text{Share price}}{\text{Book value/share}} = \frac{\$22.50}{\$11.25} = 2 \text{ times}$$

Naturally the answer is also 2 times.

However neither the total or per share calculation of market to book identify the factors that drive the market/book ratio. To see these drivers we must look to another set of relationships.

The ROE figure tells us the rate of return that the company is delivering to the shareholders (internal return). The earnings yield figure is the rate of return investors require to hold the share (required return). As a recap these two ratios are calculated as follows:

$$\text{Return on equity (ROE): } \frac{\text{EAT}}{\text{Owners' funds}} = \frac{\$60\text{m}}{\$360\text{m}} = 16.7\%$$

$$\text{Earnings yield: } \frac{\text{EPS}}{\text{Share price}} = \frac{\$1.875}{\$22.50} = 8.3\%$$

The market/book ratio falls out of the relationship between ROE (internal return) and earnings yield (required return):

$$\text{Internal return v. required return: } \frac{\text{ROE}}{\text{Earnings yield}} = \frac{16.7\%}{8.3\%} = 2 \text{ times}$$

The market to book ratio is driven by ROE. It is determined by the relationship between what the market demands (earnings yield/required return) and what the company delivers (ROE/ internal return).

This concept is of crucial importance. It illustrates the fact that investors decide on a rate of return necessary for a particular business. Then they value that business at a premium or a discount, depending on whether the return delivered by the business is greater or less than their required rate.

The importance of ROE

ROE drives company value. There are those who will dispute this statement. With good logic they will argue this is too simple an explanation because ROE is a short-term accounting measure. It does not take into account any future changes to the business or growth prospects. Nevertheless we can say that, other things being equal, *the most important driver of value is ROE.*

The V chart, covered earlier, demonstrated the key drivers of ROE. The most important are:

- ROTA
- leverage (the debt/equity ratio).

In turn, as covered in Chapter 6 on performance drivers, the factors that drive ROTA are:

- profit margin
- asset turnover.

Driving profit margin asset turnover are all the operating ratios.

So it is ROE that brings together all the operating and financing characteristics of the business.

We therefore can trace a path from the shop floor to stock-market value.

However we need to examine a little more the factors that help the stock market decide on the earnings yield it will demand from a particular company.

Investors will weigh up the prospects for:

▪ the particular company

▪ the industrial sector

▪ the economy overall.

The main influencing factors under each heading are shown in Figure 12.4.

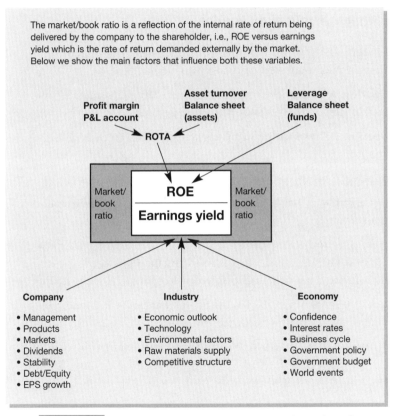

Figure 12.4 The importance of the return on equity ratio and earnings yield relationship

Investors are buying the expected future returns of the company. If growth prospects are good this will promise high returns.

However they trade off risk against return. For a high perceived risk they will look for a high return.

Note: An increase in leverage (the debt/equity ratio) has a double effect: it increases ROE but it also increases risk and therefore normally results in a higher 'earnings yield' value. The increase in ROE (the numerator) should increase corporate value but if debt/equity is pushed beyond a prudent level the resulting increase in the earnings yield (the denominator) will actually reduce overall value.

The corporate valuation model

In Figure 12.5 we are now able to pull together the various sections of the overall corporate valuation model.

Section A illustrates the drivers of operating performance covered in Part Two of this book (Chapters 5 and 6).

Section B shows the financial leverage model given earlier in this chapter.

Section C brings in the investor ratios covered in Chapter 11.

This completes the chain linking shop-floor value drivers to stock-market value.

Figures from the Example Co. plc accounts are used for the various nodes in the model. There is an arithmetical link between each node in the chain that produces the final corporate value of $720m.

The independent variables in the model that can be influenced by management can now be identified:

- the cost percentages in the profit and loss account:
    — material
    — labour
    — overheads.
- the main asset groups in the balance sheet:
    — fixed assets
    — inventories
    — accounts receivable.

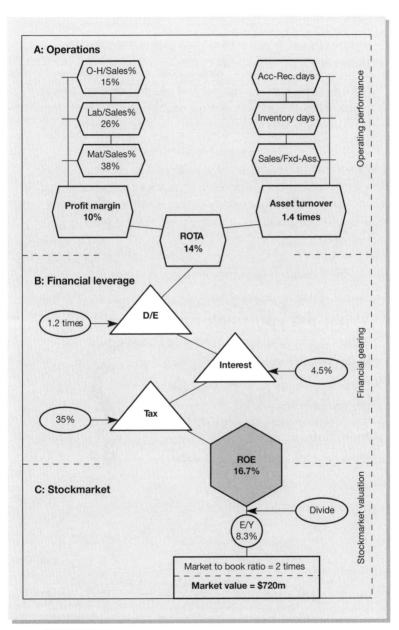

Figure 12.5 Overall corporate valuation model for the Example Co. plc

- the level of financial leverage (debt to equity ratio)
- the interest rate as well as free versus paid borrowings
- the tax rate.

One can work back from a desired end result to determine what the value of any single input variable must be, if the other inputs remain constant. This uses the equation established with the V chart.

For example, if the management of Example Co. plc set a target of 20% for ROE (post-tax), they could work back to determine that the value of ROTA needed to deliver that is 16.5%. They can subsequently set targets for each of the supporting drivers to work back to a ROTA of 16.5%.

What did you think of this book?

We're really keen to hear from you about this book, so that we can make our publishing even better.

Please log on to the following website and leave us your feedback.

It will only take a few minutes and your thoughts are invaluable to us.

www.pearsoned.co.uk/bookfeedback

Ten useful books to read next

1. *25 Need-to-Know Key Performance Indicators* by Bernard Marr (Pearson, 2014)

   This book is part of the same series as *25 Need-to-Know Management Ratios*. It is a superb complement as it largely focuses on non-financial performance measures. Used alongside the financial ratios covered in this book it is an essential part of every manager's toolkit.

2. *Key Management Ratios: The 100+ Ratios Every Manager Needs To Know* by Ciaran Walsh (Pearson, 2008).

   As well as the 25 ratios covered here, this book covers many more whilst looking at these concepts in further depth. The concept of valuation is explored further with shareholder value analysis and acquisition accounting. There is a useful section on management decision making which looks at some internal ratios including those used for project appraisal. The concluding chapter on the integrity of accounting statements is particularly useful.

3. *Ratios Made Simple: A Beginner's Guide to the Key Financial Ratios* by Robert Leach (Harriman House Ltd, 2010)

   Despite the title this is an excellent follow-up book to *25 Need-to-Know Management Ratios*. It looks at many of the same ratios as well as other ratios in further depth. It is focused on investors versus business managers. However, understanding a business from the perspective of its investors is useful for any senior manager.

4. *Finance Basics – Collins Business Secrets* by Stuart Warner (HarperCollins, 2010)

   This book contains 50 *secrets* that will help you get to grips with finance basics. From students interested in business finance to chief executives who want to know more, this book explores reading financial statements, analysing business performance, estimating business value, making profit and improving cash flow. It is a useful complement to *25 Need-to-Know Management Ratios*.

5. *Accounts Demystified: The Astonishingly Simple Guide to Accounting* by Anthony Rice (Prentice Hall, 2011)

A well explained and simple guide to the fundamental principles of accounting, currently in its sixth edition. This book is focused on those without a financial background. Very useful for managers wishing to understand the accounts on which ratios are based.

6. *How to Read a Financial Report: Wringing Vital Signs out of the Numbers* by John A. Tracy and Tage Tracy (John Wiley & Sons, 2014)

This bestselling book first published in 1979 is currently in its eighth edition. Although focused on the US, the concepts covered are relevant to an international audience. It is very good at interpreting the connections between the three key financial statements.

7. *Financial Ratios: How To Use Financial Ratios To Maximise Value and Success For Your Business* by Richard Bull (CIMA Publishing, 2007)

This book provides an in-depth insight into financial ratios. It will appeal to those who value illustrative models like those used in *25 Need-to-Know Management Ratios*. This book uses the Enterprise Stewardship Model to illustrate the power and the limitations of financial ratios. The book also includes a supporting interactive CD.

8. *Business Finance for Managers: An Essential Guide to Planning, Control and Decision Making* by Ray Fitzgerald (Kogan Page, 2002)

A well written practical guide to financial decision making with an emphasis on application versus theory. The book is designed for people from non-accounting backgrounds. Although last published in 2002, it covers perpetual principles still relevant today.

9. *Essentials of Accounting* by Leslie K. Breitner and Robert N. Anthony (Pearson Education, 2012)

An interactive workbook which provides a self-teaching and self-paced introduction to financial accounting for those wishing to look at the topic in more depth. There is an optional accompanying book by the same authors.

10. *Financial Accounting: An International Introduction* by David Alexander and Christopher Nobes (Pearson, 2013)

Although marketed as 'an introductory book to anyone with little prior knowledge or new to this subject area', this book is a comprehensive guide to financial accounting. It is an excellent book for anyone wishing to explore financial accounting in depth. A popular resource for both undergraduate and postgraduate (MBA) students.

Glossary

All items in italics are defined elsewhere in the glossary

Acid test See *quick ratio.*

Activity ratios These measure the relationship between key assets and sales. They express how well assets are being utilised. For instance, 'accounts receivable days' (see *debtor days*) shows how long cash is tied up in accounts receivable; likewise *inventory days.* We use the *sales to fixed assets* ratio to give a measure of the output being generated by major fixed assets. The term 'asset utilisation ratios' is also used in this context.

Amortisation of loan The repayment of a loan by equal periodic payments that include both interest on outstanding balance plus some repayment of principal.

Asset backing Also known as 'asset value per share', it is calculated by dividing total ordinary funds in the balance sheet by the number of issued ordinary shares.

Asset utilisation ratios See *activity ratios.*

Asset value per share See *asset backing.*

Authorised share capital The maximum value of share capital that can be issued. It is specified in the company's articles and can be increased only by permission of the shareholders.

Average collection period As *debtor days.*

Average interest rate paid The apparent rate of interest paid on loans, calculated by expressing the interest charge in the profit and loss account as a percentage of loan funds in the balance sheet. It must be kept in mind that loans at the balance sheet date may not be a true reflection of the average over the year.

Bear Term for an investor who anticipates a falling market in financial securities. This investor may sell securities not owned in order to profit from the expected drop in price. See also *bull*.

Bond US term for medium- to long-term loan. Legally it is the certificate that gives the holder the right to periodic interest payments and repayment of principal.

Bonus issue New equity shares issued from reserves and given free to company shareholders in proportion to their existing share holdings.

Book value per share The value of a share based on the balance sheet values. See also *asset backing*.

Borrowing ratio Long-term plus short-term loans expressed as a percentage of ordinary funds plus preference shares less intangibles.

Bull An investor who anticipates a rise in the price level of financial securities. This investor may purchase securities with the intention of resale before the time for settlement is due. See also *bear*.

Bullet A single payment of the total amount of a loan at the end of the period (as opposed to periodic payments during its life).

Capital employed The total of the long-term funds in the balance sheet. It includes shareholders' funds, long-term loans, preference shares, minority interests and miscellaneous long-term funds. It can also be expressed as total assets less current liabilities.

Capital market The financial market for long-term securities.

Capital reserves Shareholders' funds that have originated from sources other than trading or the nominal value of new issues.

Capital structure The mix of financing in a company. It usually refers to the proportions of debt and equity in the balance sheet.

Cash cycle A model of working capital cash flow that identifies the time required for cash paid out for raw materials and expenses to come back in from accounts receivable.

Cash flow per share Profit after interest, tax, minority and preference dividends plus depreciation divided by the number of shares.

Certificate of deposit (CD) A short-term negotiable certificate issued by a bank as evidence of a deposit that is repayable on a fixed date. It is a highly liquid bearer instrument.

Collateral A physical or financial asset used as security for a loan.

Commercial paper Loan notes issued by high-credit corporations to raise short-term funds direct from the money markets rather than from a lending institution.

Common size financial statements Statements that have been standardised by having each component expressed as a percentage of sales or total assets.

Compensating balance The minimum amount by which a company must stay in credit on a deposit account under the terms of a loan.

Covenant, restrictive A clause in a loan agreement to restrict the freedom of the borrower to act in a way that would weaken the position of the lender, such as increasing the amount of the dividend.

Credit period The number of days' sales represented by the accounts receivable. It corresponds to the term *debtor days*.

Current assets The sum of inventories, accounts receivable, cash and cash equivalents and miscellaneous short-term assets.

Current liabilities The sum of accounts payable, short-term loans and miscellaneous accruals all due for repayment within one year.

Debenture A legal document that acknowledges a loan. In the US, the term refers to an unsecured loan. In the UK it may be secured by a fixed or floating charge on the assets.

Debtor days, or, accounts receivable days The figure for trade debtors in the balance sheet is divided by the average sales per day to express the average number of days' credit taken by customers.

Debt to equity ratio The principal measure of the mix of funds in a company's balance sheet. It can be expressed in a number of different ways. The most common way is to calculate the percentage that total interest-bearing debt bears to ordinary plus preference shareholders' funds.

Debt to total assets ratio One of the debt to equity measures. Long-term loans plus current liabilities are expressed as a percentage of total assets.

Departmental ratios The effectiveness of the major departments can be assessed by using an approach similar to that for the total operation, as illustrated in Chapter 6 on performance drivers. For each department, costs and assets classified under selected headings are related to sales, cost of sales or standard hours of work produced as appropriate. Suggested ratios for Marketing and Production are shown below:

- Marketing: cost to sales ratios

    salaries and commission

    travel expenses

    advertising costs

    sales office costs

- Marketing: assets to sales ratios

  fixed assets: office

  fixed assets: cars/equipment

  finished goods

  accounts receivable

- Production: cost to cost of sales ratios

  direct material

  direct labour

  overtime

  indirect labour

  maintenance

  production planning

  supervision and so on

- Production: assets to cost of sales ratios

  fixed assets: factory premises

  fixed assets: plant

  fixed assets: vehicles

  raw material

  work in progress.

Dilution The reduction in the *earnings per share* value due to an increase in the number of shares issued or contracted to be issued in the future.

Dividend cover Expresses the number of times that dividends to the ordinary shareholders are covered by earnings. See also *payout ratio.*

Dividend per share (DPS) The actual dividend paid on each ordinary share. It can be calculated from the accounts by dividing the total ordinary dividend by the number of ordinary shares.

Dividend yield Actual dividend per share expressed as a percentage of the current share price. In the UK, imputed tax is added to dividends paid and the calculation gives gross dividend yield.

Earnings per share (EPS) The profit earned for the ordinary shareholders as shown in the profit and loss account is divided by the number of issued ordinary shares to give earnings per share. (To be strictly orthodox, the weighted average number of shares should be used.)

Earnings yield Earnings per share expressed as a percentage of the current share price. In the UK, imputed tax is added to earnings to give gross yield.

EBITDA Earnings before interest, tax, depreciation and amortisation

Employee ratios To measure the productivity of labour, three major variables – sales, profits and assets – are related back to the number of employees and their remuneration. The principal ratios used are:

- remuneration to employee
- sales to employee
- sales to remuneration
- profit to employee
- profit to remuneration
- fixed assets to employee
- working capital to employee.

Equity gearing Common funds plus preference shares expressed as percentage of long-term loan plus current liabilities.

Factoring A method of raising funds by the selling of trade debtors.

Fixed assets Land and buildings, plant and equipment and other long-term physical assets on which the operations of the company depend.

Fixed cost A type of cost where the total expenditure does not vary with the level of activity or output.

Floating rate note (FRN) Loan on which the interest rate varies with prevailing short-term market rates.

Free borrowing percentage The percentage of non-equity funds that is made up of 'free' debt, that is accounts payable, accruals and deferred tax.

Gearing A relationship between different types of funds in a company, such as loans and equity. The higher the amount of loan funds the higher the amount of fixed interest charge in the profit and loss account. Where interest charges are high, a small change in operating profit will have a much increased result in return to the equity for shareholders.

Gilts The term 'gilt-edged' refers to government longer-term borrowing instruments. They are described as 'short' where the maturity is up to five years, 'medium' for periods of five to 15 years and 'long' for over 15 years to infinity.

Intangible assets Long-term non-physical assets in the balance sheet such as goodwill and brand values.

Interest cover A liquidity ratio that expresses the number of times the interest charged in the profit and loss account is covered by profit before interest and tax.

Inventory days The inventory value in the balance sheet is expressed in terms of days. The divisor is usually the average daily cost of sales. Separate calculations are made for raw materials, work in progress and finished goods. Sometimes referred to as stock days.

Investments Investments in subsidiary and associated companies and other long-term financial assets.

Lease finance versus lease A lease under which the lessee assumes all the risks and rewards of ownership. It extends over the estimated economic life of the assets and cannot easily be cancelled. Under current accounting rules, such a lease is treated as a loan.

Leverage See *gearing*.

Leveraged buy-out The acquisition of a firm by using large amounts of debt.

LIBOR London InterBank Offered Rate – the rate at which major banks in the short-term money market lend to each other. It is a benchmark for many international loans and floating-rate issues to corporations.

Liquidity The ability to provide cash to meet day-to-day needs as they arise.

Long-term loans (LTL) Bank and other loans of more than one year.

Market capitalisation The notional total market value of a company calculated from the latest quoted market price of the share multiplied by the number of shares. The quoted price may not give an accurate value for the total shares, it may refer to only one small block of shares.

Market to book ratio The relationship between the balance sheet value of the ordinary shares and their market value. The expression 'price to book' is also used.

Matching principle A rule that a firm should match short-term uses of funds with short-term sources and long-term uses with long-term sources.

Minority interests The book value of shares in a subsidiary that are owned by members who are not shareholders of the parent company.

Miscellaneous current assets Sundry receivables and pre-payments due for realisation within one year.

Miscellaneous long-term funds A composite entry in the balance sheet that may include deferred tax, unamortised government grants, provision for pensions and so on.

Net working capital See *working capital.*

Net worth (NW) The sum of common ordinary shares plus all reserves plus preference shares less intangible assets.

Off-balance sheet A term that refers to borrowing that does not appear on the balance sheet. Sometimes achieved by a finance lease that gives the lessee all the risks and rewards, but not the legal status, of ownership.

Optimal capital structure The point at which the cost of capital to a company is reduced to the minimum by the best mix of debt and equity.

Overtrading A company is in an overtrading situation when there is not sufficient *liquidity* to meet comfortably the day-to-day cash needs of the existing level of business. There is constant danger of bankruptcy, even though the company may be trading profitably. Such a situation can come about because of past trading losses, excessive expansion and so on, but can be cured by the injection of long-term funds or, maybe, the sale of fixed assets.

Owners' funds (OF) The sum of the issued shares, capital reserves and revenue reserves. The total represents the assets remaining to the shareholders after all prior claims have been satisfied.

Paid borrowing percentage The percentage of non-equity funds consisting of interest-bearing debt.

Par value A notional value assigned to a share largely for accounting purposes.

Payout ratio The percentage of earnings available for distribution that is paid out in dividends. This ratio is the reciprocal of *dividend cover.*

Preference capital Shares that have preferential rights over common shares. These rights normally relate to distribution of dividends and repayment of capital. The shares usually carry a fixed dividend but also carry very little voting power.

Preferred creditors Creditors who, in an insolvency, have a statutory right to be paid in full before any other claims. Employees who have pay due to them would normally be in this category.

Price to earnings multiple (PE) The value derived by dividing the current share price by the *earnings per share*. Latest reported earnings or prospective earnings for the coming year may be used in the calculation.

Profit after tax (PAT) Profit available for the shareholders after interest and tax has been deducted.

Profit before interest and tax (PBIT) Operating profit plus other income.

Profit before interest, tax and depreciation (PBITD) This value corresponds very closely to cash flow from trading. See also *EBITDA*.

Profit before tax (PBT) Operating profit plus other income less total interest charged.

Quick ratio (acid test) A short-term liquidity ratio calculated by dividing current assets less inventories by current liabilities.

Retained earnings (RE) The final figure from the profit and loss account that is transferred to reserves in the balance sheet.

Return on assets (ROA) Profit before interest and tax as percentage of total assets. The corresponding term used in this book is return on total assets.

Return on capital employed (ROCE) Capital employed includes all the long-term funds in the balance sheet, that is shareholders' funds plus long-term loan plus miscellaneous long-term funds. Profit before tax is often expressed as a percentage of this to give return on capital employed. However, as the denominator includes long-term loan, the corresponding interest on these loans should be added back into the numerator.

Return on equity (ROE) A measure of the percentage return generated by a company for the equity shareholders. It is calculated by expressing profit after tax as a percentage of shareholders' funds (Where preference shares exist, they should first be deducted from shareholders' funds and the preference dividends should also be deducted from the profit figure.)

Return on investment (ROI) A term that is very widely used in connection with the performance of a company or project. It is calculated in many different ways. Usually a pre-tax profit figure is expressed as a percentage of either the long-term funds or the total funds in the balance sheet.

Return on total assets (ROTA) Profit before interest and tax expressed as a percentage of total assets.

Revenue reserves Increases in shareholders' funds that have arisen from retained profits and are available for distribution as dividends.

Rights issue A new issue of shares made by a company to its existing shareholders at a price below the current market value.

Sales to fixed assets (times) An activity and performance ratio, calculated by dividing the net fixed assets value in the balance sheet into the sales turnover figure.

Senior debt Debt that ranks ahead of junior, or subordinated debt in the event of a liquidation. See *subordinated debt.*

Share premium The difference between a share's nominal value and its sale price.

Shareholders' funds Issued ordinary shares plus reserves plus preference shares.

Short-term loans (STL) The bank overdraft, current portion of long-term debt and other interest-bearing liabilities due within one year.

Spontaneous financing Short-term financing that automatically results from the normal operations of the business. Creditors/accounts payable and certain accruals are the main sources.

Subordinated debt Debt that ranks for repayment after *senior debt.*

Subsidiaries A company is a subsidiary of another if the other owns more than 50% of the equity or effectively controls the company by means of voting shares or composition of the board of directors.

Sundry accruals An entry in the current liabilities section of the balance sheet that includes sundry accounts payable plus accrued dividends, interest, tax plus other accruals.

Tangible assets The total of all assets in the balance sheet less intangibles, such as goodwill.

Tax rate The apparent rate of tax on profit found by expressing tax charged in the accounts as a percentage of profit before tax.

Term loan Usually a medium-term loan (three to seven years) repaid in fixed, periodic instalments that cover both interest and principal over the life of the loan.

Total assets The sum of fixed assets plus intangibles plus investments plus current assets.

Treasury stock Ordinary or common shares that have been repurchased by the company.

Variable costs A type of cost where the total expenditure varies in proportion to activity or output.

Window dressing The alteration of financial statements at the time of publication to give an artificially improved appearance to the company situation. For instance, the temporary sale of inventories to a bank with agreement to repurchase could give an enhanced view of company liquidity.

Working capital The excess of current assets over current liabilities.

Working capital days The length of the working capital cycle is often calculated as inventories plus accounts receivable less accounts payable days.

Working capital to sales A liquidity ratio that is calculated by expressing working capital as a percentage of sales.

Index